KU-757-857

THE PERSONAL DEVELOPMENT GROUP

The Students' Guide

Chris Rose

KARNAC

First published in 2008 by
Karnac Books Ltd
118 Finchley Road, London NW3 5HT

Copyright © 2008 by Chris Rose

The rights of Chris Rose to be identified as the author of this work
have been asserted in accordance with §§ 77 and 78 of the Copyright
Design and Patents Act 1988.

All rights reserved. No part of this publication may be reproduced,
stored in a retrieval system, or transmitted, in any form or by any
means, electronic, mechanical, photocopying, recording, or
otherwise, without the prior written permission of the publisher.

British Library Cataloguing in Publication Data
A.C.I.P. for this book is available from the British Library

ISBN-13: 978–1–85575–535–2

Edited, designed, and produced by
Florence Production Ltd, Stoodleigh, Devon
www.florenceproduction.co.uk

Printed in Great Britain
www.karnacbooks.com

CONTENTS

ABOUT THE AUTHOR

Chris Rose is a psychotherapist and group analyst working in private practice, the NHS and the higher education sector.

She has many years experience in the training of counsellors and psychotherapists, as teacher, group facilitator, supervisor, course director and staff consultant.

Her interests lie in the relationship between group and individual, in language and communication, and in gender and social class. Her current work looks at the development of self-reflexivity, and she has published articles in *Therapy Today* and *Group Analysis*.

ACKNOWLEDGEMENTS

The experiences and ideas that have inspired this book have come from many different groups of students, trainers, counsellors, psychotherapists, patients and clients. Every group member and facilitator has made a contribution, and I am grateful to all of them for the part they have played in shaping this book. The characters in the vignettes, however, are fictitious, created from a mixture of experience and imagination.

The training courses at City College Coventry, Birmingham University, Solihull College, Coventry and Warwick University, and the Turvey Centre for Group Psychotherapy have all, in different ways, contributed to the writing of this book.

Some of the ideas have developed out of articles that I have written for the BACP publication, *Therapy Today* and its predecessor, *The Counselling and Psychotherapy Journal*. I would like to thank the editors, Sarah Browne and Eleanor Fitzpatrick, for their support and encouragement, as well as Anne Doyle, Sandra Harrison and Richard Worsley.

CHAPTER ONE

Why "personal development"?

Why should counsellors and psychotherapists spend time and effort in looking at their own attitudes and behaviours? Their work will revolve around others, not themselves, so what is the point of this self-examination? Would it not be better to spend the time learning more about other people, or developing useful skills and techniques?

These are questions that never go away, because each new generation of counselling and psychotherapy trainees has to find their own answers. They will be given a variety of ready made answers from their particular brand of training, but in the end, they have to make up their own minds. They will have to choose where to position themselves on a spectrum that extends from the "white coat" to the "intersubjective" model. At one end, therapeutic change is achieved by skilled intervention from a qualified expert. At the other, change comes about through meaningful contact between human beings.

Any sort of therapy that values the relationship between the client and the therapist/counsellor has to look at both ends of the relationship. If therapeutic change is the outcome of a relationship between two or more people, then it is neither logical nor ethical to suppose that the person labelled the therapist is a neutral ingredient. How we are as people affects the relationships we have with those we work with. This is the fundamental idea that underpins this book.

Those who are open to this approach recognise the need to know as much as they can about themselves and how they are in relationship with others. How to achieve this, however, may not be so obvious. It is possibly the most difficult aspect of training, and both trainees and trainers can struggle to find ways of accessing and promoting growth at this personal level. Creating a designated space in the time table and putting students together into a group with the task of "personally developing" may be a first step, but it certainly does not guarantee the desired outcome. If the group is to become a place in which students can genuinely learn about themselves and others, then more is required.

Some of these necessary further ingredients may need to come from the course, such as devoting time and effort to thinking through coherent and transparent policies about the relationship of the group to the course as a whole and its role in assessment. Other vital ingredients are to be found in the group itself, in both its both members and facilitator.

The role of the facilitator is complex and the manner is which it is performed is highly influential in the development of the group. It is not, however, the most significant factor in determining whether or not a group works well. This comes down to the mixture of group members, their attitudes and experiences, and their openness to genuine exploration. A skilful, competent, sensitive facilitator cannot produce a functioning group without the cooperation of the group members. Every group member has a shared responsibility to create a PD group that provides opportunities to learn and grow. This book has been written to encourage and help the open-minded student to take up that responsibility. To that end, the role of the facilitator is deliberately minimised, and the focus placed upon helping the group members to make the best of the group experience regardless of who is sitting in the facilitator's chair.

Working hard in the PD group is never enough on its own. Learning to understand and think about oneself requires a great deal more than an hour or so a week, term time only. It involves a commitment on the part of the students to take themselves very seriously indeed. That does not mean some dull earnestness, but rather a lively questioning of what we think we know about ourselves. We have ideas and pictures of who we are, what we are like, how we behave and how we relate that will all need revising in the course of personal development. Taking oneself seriously means being alive to more possibilities than we had imagined and respecting our own capacity for creativity and flexibility.

Although much of the work involves what might seem like interminable questioning, there is a large part to be played by humour. Being able to both take ourselves seriously AND recognise when we are inflating our self-importance is a major achievement in this sort of venture. Laughter can have many meanings, but in its compassionate form can transform many grey moments, especially in the PD group.

Being serious and having fun all at the same time is another of those paradoxes that are encountered again and again both in groups and in this book. In its very best version, the PD group can be hard work and at times very destabilising, but also enjoyable.

Theoretical models

The PD group is found in many different places, from clinical psychology doctorates to counselling certificates. It is always situated within a particular tribe of counsellors, psychotherapists, or psychologists who have a preferred model of how people and therapy work. Models include person centred, gestalt, existential, transpersonal, psychodynamic, humanistic, relational, systemic, cognitive-behavioural, cognitive analytic, to name but a few—and integrative of course.

Despite this variety of contexts, every course that has a PD group thereby acknowledges that the "person" of the counsellor/therapist/psychologist is a significant factor. Whatever the differences between models, the common ground lies in the belief that good practice requires self-understanding on the part of the practitioner. The task of facilitating this self-understanding unites rather than divides models. It is the common ground that brings together the clinical psychology doctorate student, the counselling certificate student, and all those other group members on different courses in different places.

Every PD group member is faced with the challenge of learning to relate in a meaningful manner, to communicate at depth, to change and to grow, and to facilitate these processes in the client. These are the common experiences that transcend the tribal boundaries of particular models and which form the basis of this book. Inevitably there will be times when this does not satisfy the purist in any model, but it is an approach that can engage a broad range of students who want to learn more both about themselves and others.

Why a group?

Some students struggle not with the idea of personal development as such, but with the group nature of the task. "I'm a private person", they say. "I could never talk openly in a group". These individuals see groups as places in which they need to protect themselves rather than expose any vulnerability. Groups can be dangerous places where members are exposed to aggression, or ridicule, or humiliation. Groups can reject, punish, attack and damage. Added to this comes the fear that groups can change behaviour, and that people behave differently in groups. As a group member I may find myself doing and saying things that seem out of character or out of my own control. The image of the mindless and violent mob comes readily to mind, with old footage of wartime rallies or contemporary street violence.

This fear of both what might be done to us and what we might find ourselves doing to others comes up again and again in conversations about groups. Being overwhelmed both from without and within seems a frightening potential that group membership might unleash. "I'm a private person" because experience has taught me that other people can dismantle my sense of who I am, break through my protective defences and expose me to intense and disturbing emotions. The ultimate danger is the loss of the "self".

This fear of who or what we could become lies at the heart of all those reasons why some people dread groups. It might not be particularly conscious, but it plays a key role in our ideas about what group membership might entail and why it should be avoided. We have an intuitive awareness that the individual may be overwhelmed by the group, and for good reason.

In our western culture, the idea of individual is given a dominant role. We emphasize self-awareness, self-regard, self esteem, self-actualising—our theoretical frameworks in counselling and psychotherapy are dominated by the individual and the intra-psychic. There is a growing awareness that this might not be the only legitimate way to conceptualise human experience, but it still exerts enormous power.

It is challenged from a variety of sources—from intersubjective theories, from group theories, and increasingly from neuropsychology and ecopsychology. But to conceptualise the human mind as an interactive phenomena and to see the "self" as inseparable from interaction with "others" requires a major intellectual effort in the pervasive Anglo-American culture. Just as physically we are encapsulated within a skin, so we conceive of ourselves psychologically as distinct and bounded. We are programmed with a view of ourselves as discrete units and of the desirability of that condition. Separation and individuation are crucial and positively valued processes, whereas merger, dependence, and enmeshment are negatively described.

With this particular version of what it is to be a human being, holding onto one's self and keeping others at a safe distance becomes a desirable goal. But the intuitive awareness of the fragility of this position and the resulting dread of group situations points to a recognition that there is another story. Our contemporary western culture and ideology may exalt the individual and downgrade the group, but the anxiety about group membership reveals the continuing power of the group.

The individual and the group

The group and the individual are mutually interdependent. The group cannot exist without the individual and the individual cannot exist without the group. Like it or not, we are group creatures. We are all born into a group, learn who we are in the context of groups and live out our lives and deaths within groups. We have no existence outside of the group—the family, the school, the club, the workplace, the society, the culture, the language, the beliefs. Even the most isolated of people are born into relationship with others, belong to the group "men" or "women", live as a member of a particular society in a particular historical context.

We think of the group as being made up of individuals, added together like so many Lego bricks. First comes the individual, then we add some of them together, and a group is created. In this version, the individual is prior to the group. But of course, when we ask where these individuals originate, the answer is a group. Individuals are fragments of groups.

The notion of the individual as a "fragment, dynamically shaped by the group" comes from the work of S.H. Foulkes,[1] a pioneer in group work. He also referred to the individual as "an artificial, if plausible, abstraction". They are challenging phrases, but if we really engage with them we can understand the relationship between group and individual in a new way.

Challenging our ingrained ways of thinking is always difficult, and requires a sustained effort. In a way, the purpose of this book is to do just that—to challenge habitual ways of thinking and to expand the understanding of human relationships. What does it mean to be a "fragment of a group"?

Think about all the groups that you have been a member of through out your life, from your first family through to your current group memberships. Groups come in many forms—work group, sports team, church, interest group, package holiday, political affiliation, extended family, school, college, and on and on. Then there are the larger groups of culture, country, gender, race, age, ability, nationality, religion, and so forth. These are groups we are inescapably part of, just as we are part of a particular historical context. The narrative of every life can be told from the perspective of group membership. Many of the groups are interrelated, circles within circles, at times concentric and at times overlapping.

Who we are, the "I", comes from a constant negotiation between the rewards and responsibilities of these myriad group memberships. The separate, autonomous, freestanding individual exists only in our cultural mythology. We are inextricably linked to each other, and we need that web of connection.

Now we can return to the question of "why a group" with a different perspective. Some might want to answer it in a practical way, seeing it as a format that is time efficient, relatively inexpensive and the best solution found so far to the problem of ensuring all students have the opportunity to engage with the task of personal development. However, there is another, more persuasive answer that takes into account the inescapable inter-relationship of group and individual. We become who we are through our group belonging. This is as true in the present as it was in the past, and if we are to change and develop, we can only do it in the context of others. The PD group offers an opportunity to experience and understand me-in-relation-to-others in a here and now context that will be shaped by all those other groups, past and present.

Communication in groups

The members of the PD group, like those in a therapy group, have to learn how to communicate with each other. All of them have learnt how to communicate in other significant groups and can speak fluently in that particular language. In certain families, for example, when mother says "I'm perfectly fine", everyone understands that the message is "I'm upset and angry because you haven't done what I wanted you to do". Or when father says "I'm busy" he means "Don't tell me how things are for you because I can't cope with how you feel."

Everyone comes into the group from a lifetime of learning about the different levels of communication, and how to send and receive signals in their own unique environment. Much of this learning is out of awareness, unconsciously absorbed in the process of living within a particular group. Trying to communicate in a group with those who have learnt different languages is one of the best ways to recognise the idiosyncrasies of one's own way of communicating.

It also challenges once again the idea that group members are separate, discrete entities that send messages to each other across the room. There will be moments in the group when emotions appear to pass mysteriously from person to person, when members find themselves thinking the same thoughts, or when the whole group is caught up in a powerful shared emotion. At these times, the boundaries between self and other appear blurred and confusing. The boundaries between self and other ARE blurred and confusing, the closer we look at the interrelationship between group and individual.

We have the capacity as human beings to communicate with each other in far more powerful ways than language. If one person yawns, then another person will yawn also in an automatic mirroring response. Something has been shared which does not rely upon language or cognition but is wired into us from birth. We have the capacity to make sense of the behaviour of others without conscious theorising, and this innate ability enables us to understand and predict aspects of our environment.

Healthy newborn babies of any race, colour, or religion have in common an astonishing ability to relate which demonstrates our fundamental intersubjectivity. As young as 18 hours old, newborns can reproduce facial gestures displayed by an adult they are facing.[2] They can translate a visual stimulus—an adult sticking their tongue out, into an equivalent physical activity. This means they have somehow solved the problem of translating what they see from the perspective of viewer into their own perspective as actor- without going through any process of consciously identifying an "other" or a "self" or even a "tongue". The newborn has no visual awareness of its own tongue, for example, so how does he or she accurately copy this movement?

The answer seems to lie in a neurological map or activity that is common to all humans. We are born with a capacity to intuitively and automatically recognise the analogy between self and other, which forms the basis for establishing all our subsequent relationships. This is the basis of empathy. Other social factors will determine its development and sophistication, but these are built upon this fundamental intersubjective mode of relating to the world.

Watching someone prick her or his finger with a needle creates the same pattern of neural activity as pricking one's own finger. The same neurons are activated in the brain of the "doer" as in the "viewer". A series of mirroring mechanisms, operating unconsciously and automatically, constantly simulates actions, emotions, and sensations. Our brains are continuously modelling the behaviour of others in the same way that they model our own behaviour.[3] Each individual is engaged in a continuous, ongoing and unconscious shared activity with the other. Even the idea of the individual as a fragment of a group now seems too boundaried and discrete. The more closely we look at the boundaries between each other, the more we become aware of the connective tissue that holds us all in place.

Above the surface we communicate by language in all its various forms—conversation, lectures, songs, messages in bottles, letters, phone calls, emails, whereas under the surface we are in a shared pool of mutual mirroring, emotion and sensation. Communication takes place through this communal matrix of experience. Here we are able to share by being in the same ocean, rather than sending messages.

In the face of these unfamiliar ways of thinking about what it is to be a person, it may be tempting to slide back into the usual simplifications that draw clear lines between what I feel and what you feel, who I am and who you are. One of the challenging features of the group, however, is its capacity to undermine these accepted wisdoms. We are who we are in relationship and can only grow and develop in the context of others.

But my training is in individual therapy. How does that fit in?

The reluctant group member might respond that they could develop better in the context of one other person rather than a group. After all, most of the PD group members are themselves training to work in one-to-one settings rather than in groups, so the argument that suggests that development requires a group context may sound unconvincing. However, a closer look at the process of individual counselling or psychotherapy may reveal the connection.

The majority of students for whom this book is written will be engaged in types of therapy that seek to improve the quality of peoples' lives in a demonstrable way. That is to say, at some point any gains that have been acquired in the counselling room will be expected to manifest themselves in the client's day-to-day existence. Any sustainable growth has to be lived out within the network of relationships that form the client's context. There are always a proportion of clients who are unable to achieve this transition and any seeds sown in one-to-one therapy, however positive, fail to germinate.

Many clients are themselves acutely aware that change is systemic, and if they change one part then others will follow. There is a common anxiety that changing behaviour or attitudes may lead to losing relationships or losing one's place in the group.

Sustainable change in one fragment of a group depends upon change in other fragments. If this does not happen, the individual reverts to the familiar styles of relating, or leaves the group in search of another that fits better with their new shape.

Growth and development on the part of the student has the same challenges. Trainees sometimes insist that they are doing the work of growth and development behind the scenes in individual therapy, and so do not need to participate in the PD group.

Individual therapy can be valuable in addressing the fears of participating in the group and can work creatively alongside the PD group experience to promote change and understanding. Unfortunately, sometimes it is used to keep the group at a safe distance, especially when the individual therapist has unaddressed fears of their own around groups. Then "group" and "individual" work are polarised into good and bad or set in competition with each other. This is a lost opportunity, for the reality is that they can work very effectively together.

The other reality is that any genuine and sustainable growth has to survive beyond the confines of a counselling room and become visible in the world. To achieve this, the trainee, like any future client, will have to renegotiate their place within their own network of significant relationships. Growth will demonstrate its presence in all sorts of visible ways, and the training course along with the PD group will feel the impact. The student who says "I'm doing this development work outside of the PD group" and shows no sign of growth inside the group will not convince anyone.

PD group or therapy group?

Does "personal development" differ from "personal therapy"? Is it possible to draw a clear line between them? Is the development group only for superficial matters whereas a therapy group would deal with really important material? Can a PD group go "too deep" and stray into the territory of therapy? Or is there really very little difference between the two? These are important and reasonable questions for any student embarking on a training course with a PD group.

There are a range of ways in which the PD group differs from a therapy group, and some aspects that it may share. The differences begin right from the start, before the group even meets.

Members of a therapy group come together for help. They have acknowledged that at this stage in their lives, they need something or someone to give them a hand. This is why they are in the group, searching for whatever it is that will improve the quality of their lives.

Therapy groups do not usually spend weeks and weeks filling up the time with the question "what are we supposed to be doing here?" in the way that PD groups can. There is a mutual recognition that everyone there has some common purpose in "getting better", whatever that may mean.

The members of a PD group are not overtly there for these reasons. Sometimes there is a sort of inverse assumption—rather than "we are all here because we need help", there is "we are all here because we want to help". Members of a therapy group have acknowledged to each other that they are vulnerable, just by their presence in the group. In the PD group members may be vulnerable also, but this is not the rationale for the group's existence.

The respective labels of "student" and of "patient" or "client" have particular associations. There is an assumption that the "student" is more psychologically robust, with more personal resources and will thereby require less nurture or containment. The course and the group facilitator do not have the same level of responsibility for the student's psychological well being that the health service and a group psychotherapist would have for a patient/client. Although there are many examples of students falling into the role of client and seeking counselling type relationships with tutors or fellow students, this is not the goal of training. In addition, the label "student" operates within a context of assessment. Although therapy group members may well have fears about "not being good enough" they are not usually writing about their ideas and experiences and having them marked. Neither are they seeking a qualification in order to develop a career. The student, however, is caught up in attainment and assessment at every turn, and this plays a major role in the PD group.

There are other differences. In a therapy group, members undergo some sort of assessment for their suitability, whereas students are assessed not for a group experience but for a place on a course. They will rarely have the time or space to explore their attitudes, likely behaviours, characteristic response, fears and anxieties about the PD group component. In comparison, the member of a therapy group has more information and more opportunity to explore their own attitudes before joining a group than a student does.

Once in the therapy group, members would usually agree to interact only when in the group. In this way every member is a witness to the interactions of every other member, and the creation of alliances within the group can be looked at and talked about. In contrast, the PD group has members who interact continually. They see each other in seminars, work groups, practical sessions, as well as maybe having lunch together and meeting up socially. There will inevitably be pairings and subgroups, with some group members having information that others do not. This gives any group the opportunity to hide away from what is really going on in its midst. In order to enable the group to develop into a place where challenges can be issued, contained and processed, members have to actively work hard not to split apart into smaller groups or pairs.

The idea of "containing" is one that will appear again and again in most training courses. For therapeutic change to take place, a client requires some sense of being held, or contained. A set time, a quiet room, a clear awareness of confidentiality, and a counsellor or therapist who is not overwhelmed or disabled by whatever information or emotion is put into the session—these are examples of containment. There are different sizes and types of containers that determine how much and what sort of things can be put in them. Six sessions of solution focused counselling will not contain the same material as two years of psychoanalytic psychotherapy.

The PD group starts out as a relatively shallow container. In comparison to the therapy group, there is less clarity about the purpose, the interactions of members are not confined to the group itself, making confidentiality harder to negotiate and maintain, and there are long holiday breaks to interrupt the work. Overall, the boundary around the PD group is less sharply defined, and hence the relatively shallow profile of the initial container. Members of a therapy group usually have the advantage of starting out with a container that is more secure, offering the possibility of relating with each other in meaningful ways, however difficult that may be. These are initial possibilities, however, and groups can develop in surprising ways.

In the end, both types of group share a fundamental common ground. Both personal development and therapy in groups rest upon the mutual and meaningful relationships that the members painstakingly build in the process of the group's existence. The reality is that members of both have to take responsibility for their own behaviour and the impact that they have upon others.

Students gain an enormous amount of self-knowledge in the supportive and challenging environments of training courses. The outcome might look very hard to distinguish from that of therapy. As always in this work, there is a paradox. Despite all the differences between a therapy group and a PD group, there are times when it is not possible to distinguish one from the other. The fly on the wall of the PD group room and the therapy group would have no idea that these were different sort of experiences if both groups were functioning well. The conversations, the emotional tensions, the struggle to relate—all would sound very similar.

Given the words "therapy" and "personal development", this is perhaps inevitable. "Development" derives from "unfold, unfurl" whereas "therapy" derives from "healing". If what is unfolding has been damaged in some way, then it may need healing in order to unfurl. Conversely, if something has been damaged, it may need to unfold before it can be healed.

Notes

1 Foulkes, S.H. and Anthony, E.J. (1984). *Group Psychotherapy: The Psychoanalytic Approach.* London: Maresfield Library, 1984 (reprint).

2 Meltzoff, A.N. and Moore, M.K. (1977). "Imitation of facial and manual gestures by human neonates". *Science*, 198: 75–8.

3 Gallese, V. "The manifold nature of interpersonal relations: the quest for a common mechanism". In: C. Frith & D. Wolpert (Eds.). *The Neuroscience of Social Interaction.* Oxford: Oxford University Press, 2003.

CHAPTER TWO

Getting on board

The search for self-knowledge and understanding has often been described as a journey, and it can be a helpful metaphor for the PD group experience. This is a journey where the other passengers are impossible to avoid, all inextricably bound together in the same boat.

Journeys can provoke both excitement and anxiety, which each student will deal with in their own characteristic style. They may try to prepare for all eventualities, or they may throw caution to the winds and just get on with it. Some people prepare for their journeys in meticulous detail, whilst others just throw a few things in a case and hope for the best. This particular sort of journey is one that can benefit from a middle way between the two extremes. Some preparation and thought before the boat sets sail can reap its rewards later on.

There are two key elements to think about. The first centres upon the nature of the particular group and the information that is available concerning it. PD groups come in a variety of sizes and formats with differing amounts of information prior to departure. Each feature of the group will play its part in the journey ahead, and can be usefully reflected upon in advance. Discovering as much as possible about the nature of the group is a valuable type of preparation, but to be really useful it needs to be supplemented by self-discovery.

This second key element is a much more personal exploration in which the challenge is to identify what you—the reader, the student—will be bringing into the group. What luggage will you be carrying on board? This is the point at which it stops being an intellectual inquiry and moves into personal learning.

What information is available?

Some courses provide written information about the PD group that sets out the nature of the group and the role it plays in the overall assessment for the course. Other courses have little written information but may discuss the group in detail at interview. Sometimes the student has very little information until the course has already begun, and sometimes there just is no information at all. Perhaps this is due to a lack of thought on the part of the course organizers, or perhaps it reflects the differing attitudes that are held towards providing students with information.

The group experience, it is argued, is unique for every student and should be left open to develop as it will. General guidelines can be misleading at best, and at worst, distort the experience by introducing expectations or ideas that would not otherwise have been in the group. Another argument would be that the anxiety produced by not knowing is a valuable and necessary energy for the group process, which although disturbing can open new possibilities for growth.

Then there is the more prosaic argument that sees little value in providing information because a) not everyone will read it, and b) those that do will have forgotten all about it as the group progresses. Learning takes place through experience, and the student will only properly understand the written material when they have the relevant experiences in the group.

Although I have some sympathy for this view, I would not be writing this book if I believed it to be entirely correct. There are limitations to learning through reading something like this, but there also some very positive gains from demystifying the group process. Being open about what we know, or what we think we know, can contribute to the success of the group—both as a way of being *within* it, and as a way of thinking *about* it.

Is the PD groupwork assessed?

This is the fundamental and problematic question, which may or may not be clearly answered in the course information. There are a range of possible answers stretching from, "no, not at all" at one end of the continuum, to "yes, and here are the criteria" at the other. In between are various formulas that try to balance the need for a confidential and secure environment within the group with the responsibilities of trainers to ensure certain standards are met. If there is no clarity, then the group itself may well spend a lot of time caught in the confusion. There is always the fear in a PD group that any disclosures of weakness and vulnerability will be heard as evidence of unsuitability to function as a counsellor or therapist. Where there is no clarity about the group's role in assessment, this can reach disabling proportions, and the boat never sets sail.

In what circumstances might material from the PD group be used as an indication of a member's unsuitability to be a counsellor or therapist? How would any information be passed on to the course team? At this point, the role of facilitator becomes very significant. Is the facilitator assessing the performance of the group and its members and passing on information to the course team? Is the whole group involved in making this sort of judgment, or is it the facilitator's responsibility alone? The fantasy and/or the reality that the facilitator is judging students will play an important part within the group. Addressing this issue, ideally through clear communications from the course as well as opportunities for discussion, will give the group a better chance of working productively.

Size and format. What type of group is it?

Is it a small, 8–12 seater group with a facilitator? Are there other small groups on the course? Does the whole group meet together at times? Or is it a large, whole course group of 20 plus, meeting together regularly? The size of the group plays an important part in the process.

Generally, if there are more than a dozen members, it gets increasingly difficult to hold onto a sense of group belonging. Often this difficulty is responded to by creating subgroups—smaller clusters that can more readily generate a sense of belonging and security. The larger group may then become very preoccupied with its internal divisions—rather like a federal nation trying to hold together powerful states that are competing with each other for resources. So that, for example, the first years vie with the second years, the ones on placement at one agency vie with another, the younger ones band together, and so on. If the group is large, security is often sought initially in the smaller unit, the subgroup.

Many courses recognize this tendency and build upon it, dividing the student group into two or more small PD groups. This structure sets up its own dynamics in which the small groups have to manage the boundary between themselves, whilst at the same time being part of the larger teaching group. Curiosity about what "really" happens in the other groups is healthy and inevitable, and can lead into potentially rich areas such as competition, envy, antagonism, feelings of deprivation or exclusion, and so forth.

If the format also provides a large group, where all the students meet, then questions have to be addressed about what is appropriately discussed where. Is it acceptable to talk in the big group about things that have happened in the small groups? Is the large group a forum for exposing difficult areas that are then despatched to the small groups for processing? Is it a place where emotional issues are largely kept to one side? Is it a place where the student body can confront the staff team? In this preparatory stage, it is helpful to have some idea of the respective purpose and function of both large and small group.

Different group formats offer different opportunities and obstacles for exploration and experience. Sometimes, the teaching group and the PD group is the same thing. The whole group meets for a specified time that is devoted to "personal development". In these circumstances the boundary between course group and PD group is one of timing alone. This particular format works very successfully in workshops and short courses. As a longer term PD group structure, size is again a critical factor. Once the group is larger than around 12, it may inhibit personal disclosure, and students may take the more intimate aspects of their personal learning into other areas—supervision, tutorials, individual counselling or therapy, for example.

Another outcome in the larger group could be the establishment of an "inner" circle, which picks up the challenge of working in a group, and an "outer" circle, which largely spectates. The other critical factor is facilitation. Is this is carried out by the teaching team or by someone from outside of the course? Is the course totally enclosed within itself or is there some outside interruption?

The facilitator

Whatever their personal style, the facilitator is the most visible and scrutinized person in the group. They may play a variety of roles— teacher, mentor, colleague, parent, friend, or enemy as the group develops. There is an unavoidable element of authority in the role of facilitator, whatever the model, and this inevitably engages with the attitudes and experiences of authority that members bring to the group. But this is all work for the group in progress.

At this preparatory stage, there is another question to be asked concerning "who" the facilitator is in terms of the overall course structure. Is the facilitator a part of the course team, or someone external to the course whose sole function is to facilitate the PD group? The two options can set up different dynamics within the group.

Generally the less identified the facilitator is with the course, the safer it can feel to bring personal vulnerabilities into the group. If the facilitator is an "outsider", then there may be more emotional security for the student to bring the "non-student" parts of themselves into the group. Of course, there are other variables at play, particularly that of assessment and feedback to the course, and this is not a guaranteed outcome.

On the other side, there can be something very attractive about the merging of tutor- facilitator roles. Having the same person or people responsible for emotional, experiential and academic teaching can draw out some very powerful feelings: perhaps it emotionally recreates a very early relationship in which one carer takes responsibility for a whole range of needs, as in the mother-infant relationship. Of course, this will have different outcomes for different students, ranging from a very positive and nurturing experience, to one that is suffocating, or persecutory and invasive.

Tutors may promote the idea that they can draw internal boundaries and not let one part of their role influence others and many do this as well as is humanly possible. From the students' perspective, however, there is the awareness that this boundary is fragile and limited. However good the tutor is at maintaining boundaries, they cannot genuinely "not have heard" something significant that has been said in their presence, whichever role they are performing at the time. For this reason, many courses operate a system where only staff that are not involved with the student year group in any other capacity will be group facilitators. In this way a more distinct boundary can be drawn between the work of personal development and taught aspects of the training.

So far the facilitator has been discussed more as a function than as an actual person. One thing that is fairly reasonable to presume is that the facilitator is either male or female. Their visible characteristics such as gender, age, ethnicity, style of dress and speech, are again all ingredients that will be part of the group right from the very beginning. Later on, more characteristics will become visible and perhaps open for discussion and reflection, and all of these elements will provoke some reaction somewhere in the group. Different trainings, models, and styles will give rise to different levels of disclosure on the part of the facilitator, but as long as the facilitator holds on to their task of "facilitating" rather than being a group member, there is always a difference between her or him and the rest of the group. This difference can prove endlessly fascinating, challenging, irritating and also productive within the work of the PD group.

The members. Who is in the group?

A homogeneous group, where members share key characteristics such as gender, race, ethnicity, age, social class, physical ability, will not work in the same way as a group in which there are multiple differences in any of these aspects. There is no such thing as a group that has no elements of difference within it, but some are more powerful, emotive, problematic and enriching than others. Our attitudes to those we perceive as "different" are rarely as politically correct as we would wish them to be, and the self reflexive student will need to work with this reality (Chapter 8).

Finding oneself to be an "only one"—the only male, the only disabled member, the only non white member, the oldest or the youngest, for example,—will have different consequences for different people, depending on their "luggage" and that of other members in the group. It is unlikely, however, to be a neutral event without feelings or consequences, and the PD group ideally will explore this. At this point it becomes increasingly difficult to separate the "intellectual information" from the emotional response, which lead us into the heart of personal development.

Luggage

It is quite possible to read all of the above and treat it as information that may or may not be useful. But if it is to be transformed into personal learning, you, the reader, the student, have to be much more involved. What impact might it have on you to find yourself sitting in a group circle of say 24 people? How would that feel? For example, in a group with 24 others you might re-experience how it was in school, or an extended family gathering, or some other event in your life.

Everyone sitting in the group brings emotions, images, and attitudes that are born of their own experiences in life up to this point. This is the luggage that hopefully can be unpacked in the course of the journey, and repacked where appropriate into a lighter and less burdensome shape.

Self reflexivity

The capacity to reflect upon one's self—attitudes, emotions, behaviour and thought—is the key ingredient in personal development. A model of counselling or psychotherapy that locates the therapeutic factors in the relationship between therapist and client has to pay attention to the therapist. The counsellor inevitably brings into the relationship their own conscious and unconscious material, and the more they know about that, the better for the client.

Relating to others at depth is inseparable from relating to oneself at depth. Our ability to think about ourselves and experience ourselves from the "inside and the outside" is crucial if we are to be able to offer this sort of relating to other people. One of the purposes of the PD group is to facilitate this ability, but it cannot be achieved in an hour and a half, once a week, term time only. It has to be supported by an ongoing internal dialogue within each student.

Take the example of Jackie, an attractive, lively young woman in her late twenties. She is enthusiastic about her new course in counselling and is determined to get the most from it. She is trying to prepare herself for the PD group, imagining what it might be like, and talks with her friend Carol, who completed a similar course a few years ago.

Carol: *So how do you feel about being in this PD group?*
Jackie: *That depends on the group, doesn't it?*
Carol: *Yes but—you are going to bring your own experiences to the group, and that will have an impact. Do you like being in a group? Can you think of a group you've enjoyed being a part of?*
J: *Mmm. Being part of the family group at Christmas when I was little— that was good. And when I was at school, in the netball team—that was fun. There were 5 of us who did everything together, and we were all in the team. But after Dad died, everything changed. Mum moved and I had to change schools, so I lost all my friends. I hated my new school, everyone was really unfriendly.*
C: *So did you feel like an outsider?*
J: *Definitely. Then when I went to university, I shared a house with 4 girls— that was another sort of group I suppose, and that was good.*
C: *And now?*
J: *Mainly it's just me and David. There's one of the girls from university who I still see now and then. Oh yes—at work there are two women in my office, I suppose we're a sort of group, we all get on ok.*
C: *So there have been some good group experiences—any bad ones?*
J: *That walking holiday where the leader flipped. He was really strange, incredibly talkative and hyper, and I kept clear of him as much as I could. Then one day we'd been walking for hours in the mountains and he was getting more and more wound up. Looking back, I realise he was completely lost and panicking, but at the time it just seemed unreal. He was screaming at us to hurry—run, run, he was shouting. It was far too dangerous to run anywhere, lots of loose scree and steep drops, and the light was going too. Then he collapsed—we all thought he was having a heart attack. Some of the group were saying we had to go back and some were insisting we should carry on. A couple were getting hysterical—it was awful, really awful ... Why am I talking to you about this? It was years and years ago ...*

At this point Jackie is surprised to find herself thinking about an earlier group experience, and the dialogue is leading her into territory that she has not been particularly aware of before. Powerful experiences are rarely exhausted without repeated revisiting and reexamining, and she has opened the door to discovering more about both this incident in her life and her relationship to groups.

The fictitious Jackie has been able to talk with a friend in this example, and it can be enormously valuable to have someone who will engage in this sort of questioning dialogue. But at some point it is necessary to learn how to talk with oneself, to question and wrestle with internal conversations.

This is the sort of self-exploration that every student can do before the group even starts. What follows is a series of questions that are worth asking before the group begins. As an example of how the exercise might be done, I have used Jackie again, this time talking with Herself.

J: What do you see as your role in the groups you belong to?

H: *In my family, I think I was the joker—until Dad died, and then I don't know. I was the only girl and I think my Mum leant a lot on me, so I became more serious—a little parent maybe. At university I think I got back into being the "good laugh" again. If I have to go to departmental meetings at work, though, I'm very quiet and never say anything.*

J: Imagine yourself sitting in the PD group. What is the worst thing that could happen?

H: *Nobody would like me—I've already thought about that. I'd be the odd one out. That would be the worst thing, being on my own in the group.*

J: How would you feel if someone was upset in the group?

H: *That would be fine—we all have to support each other, I think.*

J: And what if someone was angry in the group?

H: *If they were angry with me, I'd hate that—probably have to leave. Or if they were angry with someone else, I'd try to protect that person. I don't like anger, it's not necessary—and we're all supposed to be caring people. Aren't we? That's why we're on this course, because we want to help people!*

J: Do you imagine that you might get angry or upset?

H: *It takes a lot to get me angry—like I said, I don't think it's a good thing at all. But being upset, yes, I can imagine talking about something important and maybe getting a bit tearful, yes.*

J: Would you feel differently in an all women group from an all
     men group?
H: *I think I'd feel quite lost in an all men group. Women are easier to talk
     to, aren't they? It's not that I don't like men—I think they're great,
     but if I was the only woman, I think it would be very hard to talk about
     myself.*

J: What if the facilitator was a man?
H: *No problem.*

J: Come on! No-one's suggesting there will be a problem, just
     asking you to reflect upon how it might feel.
H: *Mmm. Maybe I would look up to him a bit, like my Dad, who I adored.
     I guess it might get me thinking more about my Dad—although I've
     already done a lot of work around his death and I've sorted it, I'm sure.*

J: And if the facilitator was a woman?
H: *Depends on how she is. I usually get on great with women—my boss
     is a woman and we have a really good relationship. Sometimes I think
     it might be a bit too close—she ends up telling me all her problems,
     but then the facilitator isn't going to do that, is she?*

And so on . . .

This is an internal dialogue that Jackie is developing and which
will be a valuable asset in the task of understanding herself.

In the example, there are several points when Jackie comes up
against something in herself that resists the question, or has an
answer that seems very inflexible. These points highlight some area
that Jackie perhaps does not understand clearly about herself, or
which disturb her in some way. These are the "sore spots" which
we all have, and which we need to be aware of and explore if genuine
personal development is to take place. It is always much easier to
see these spots in someone else. You will probably identify them
readily in the PD group, across the circle. Recognizing them in oneself
takes more effort.

If we look at Jackie's conversations, there are several interesting
observations that can be made. For instance, it looks as if the death
of her father radically disrupted her experiences of belonging in
groups. The walking incident echoed this is a way when the male
leader collapsed and the holiday was ruined. All the other groups

she mentions seem to be women only groups. It is possible that at some level Jackie's experiences have led to her to perceive that men will let you down.

Now imagine a scene at some stage in the life of the PD group where the male facilitator is off sick for 3 weeks. Jackie's emotional reactions to this are likely to be coloured by her previous experiences of male vulnerability and unreliability. If she can explore and link her present reactions and the underlying past experiences in the group, then is she is on the way to becoming a self-reflective practitioner. If she has been able to recognise some of this before the group starts, then Jackie can actively use the group to explore and challenge her own preconceptions about reliability, vulnerability and gender.

In many course, students are expected to keep a journal about their learning—academic and personal. The journal is another form of internal dialogue, helping to express oneself and also to "hear oneself" talk or think in the way that a therapist might do. It is a very helpful way of trying to sort out the luggage, and also to recognise the "sore spots". Even if it is not a course requirement, it is worth thinking about writing down or recording your own internal conversations, which are provoked by the personal development work. Developing an internal dialogue will complement the work in the PD group by opening more paths to self-discovery.

Try it out. Here is a set of questions similar to the ones that Jackie was working with. The task is to answer them as fully and openly as you can. If you record the conversation with yourself on tape, or write it down, you will then have the opportunity to look at it again at a later date with more sense of distance. You might find some things of interest here, too. The important thing is to be interested, not critical. Remember that you are looking for pieces in a jigsaw puzzle, not conducting a criminal investigation!

These first two questions relate to your history as a group member. We have already begun to look at the group nature of life (Chapter 1) and the ways in which we are shaped by, and shape, our group experiences. Look back at your experiences in the different groups that you are or have been a member of.

1. What sort of group member are you? What part do you play? Do you behave differently in different groups, or do you have a fairly consistent pattern?

The following list is to help you think, but is not exhaustive. You may come up with other patterns.

Joker	Guru	Conciliator	Rescuer	Rebel
Leader	Observer	Competitor	Deviant	Outsider
Facilitator	Carer	Martyr	Teacher	Servant

2. Think about positive and negative experiences that you have had in groups. Talk with yourself about them. What were the ingredients that contributed to their positive or negative feel? Was it size, membership, leadership, task, context—or something else that you can identify?

The next set of questions relate specifically to the PD group.

1. Imagine yourself sitting in the PD group. What is the worst thing that could happen?
2. How would you feel if strong emotions were expressed in the group? Would you find some emotions more difficult to deal with than others?
3. Can you envisage being angry or upset in the group yourself? What do you imagine might trigger this?
4. What would be the most difficult issues to discuss in the group?
5. Look back at your responses to the questions about your past. How might these aspects reveal themselves in the PD group? Think of a possible scenario where this might happen.

The final questions concern your own concept of personal development.

1. What difference would you like to see between yourself as you are now, and the person you might become at the end of the PD group?
2. How would this show itself in your life? What would you do differently?

If you set sail as a "carer" in the group, for example, what other parts will you be playing by the time the group ends? Growth involves change, and change involves anxiety. It is helpful right at the outset to reflect upon how any desired change will actually affect behaviour. If nothing else, you might recognize some ambivalence, which is another important piece of luggage that you carry with you into the group.

CHAPTER THREE

Setting off

The first group meeting will vary widely according to the particular course, students and facilitator. For most students, however, there is a common theme, and that is anxiety. It comes in different intensities, from sheer panic to slight apprehension, and is displayed in different forms—talking too much, not speaking, fidgeting, feeling sick, needing the windows open, and so on. In its less extreme versions, anxiety is a healthy and positive response when setting off on this unpredictable journey. There are weighty expectations of self-disclosure, openness, authenticity, directness and challenge—often very threatening experiences in relationships.

The few who do not experience anxiety at this point are those who are confident that they can keep themselves safe on this journey, and that nothing will seriously disturb their internal world. The obvious problem here is that it is only when our internal worlds are disturbed that we genuinely learn anything. Established patterns have to be shaken up if there is to be space for anything new. It is more hopeful to start from a place of apprehension than confidence, because that is to take seriously the possibility of disturbance and change. It also recognises that groups are powerful places and have the potential to be destructive as well as enormously creative. (Chapter 1) It is realistic to set out with some trepidation.

So what can the student expect right at the start? Groups, like boats, are launched in different styles.

Starting at the quayside

Carol sat next to Debbie, someone she had already discovered she felt comfortable with. They were in the same room that was used for the teaching, and had set the chairs out in a circle themselves at the request of the tutor. The facilitator arrived with a cheerful "hello". They had met him briefly on the previous weekend's introductory session. He began by asking them to go round the circle, saying something about themselves. (They had already done this in the earlier teaching session, although nobody said this.) The elderly woman in the group began with quite a lengthy account of her job, her family and their pets. She set the pattern and everyone followed suit, so it was taking some time to hear everyone's self-description.

All eyes were on the facilitator who then offered to say a little about himself if the group were interested. Lots of nods around the circle indicated that the group were indeed interested. He had just begun to describe where he worked and what he did when two students arrived with a cheery "Hi". He sympathised with their complaint about the lack of time between teaching sessions and the PD group, and then began again. He finished by saying how important it was that everyone in the group felt able to be open with each other, and that he hoped to be open with them.

By now, Carol was feeling quite comfortable. It didn't seem too different from the morning's teaching session. Then a large, flamboyantly dressed woman asked the facilitator how much experience he had had in facilitating PD groups. It turned out that this was only the second group that he had worked with—"so I'm learning just like you", he said. Carol thought he seemed anxious at this point and wanted to reassure him somehow, but the only male student in the group was telling the group that he himself had had a lot of experience in leading groups within his company—different sort of groups, naturally, but none the less, valuable experience which the group might want to call upon.

The facilitator thanked him for that, and then went on to suggest that they might like to spend some time thinking about what ground rules they wanted to have in the group. One of the students who had been late said that she didn't want it to be a group where people "just took out their angry feelings on each other". Carol agreed, but the man in the group wanted to clarify this. "Does that mean we can't express any anger in this group? What if we feel angry? Aren't we supposed to be open about our feelings?"

Carol felt irritated with him. The flamboyant woman said she had been in a PD group before, and people had got very angry with each other. It *had been unpleasant and one group member had left. She asked the facilitator what he thought. He said he thought one possible ground rule might be that everyone treated each other respectfully.*

"I think we would need to clarify what we meant by respectfully", said the man.

A woman with greenish hair who hadn't spoken before said, "Yeah, I don't want to have to be nice to everyone all the time."

Carol thought she'd much rather be in a group where people were nice to each other all the time than one where there were open displays of anger, but she said nothing.

This boat is bobbing alongside the quay whilst the group think about what would make it safe to set sail. There is a sense that this could take some time as, already, differences are emerging and the water is not entirely calm. Establishing ground rules right at the start is a very common opening move, which at times pays dividends later on in the journey.

In the next example, the group starts in a very different manner.

Starting with a splash

Carol sat next to Debbie, someone she had already spoken to a few times, and felt comfortable with. The room was at the end of a long gloomy corridor, and looked shabby and untidy. The chairs had been set out in a circle before they arrived, but no-one, Carol noticed, had cleared away the half empty paper mugs from the tables pushed to the back. Most of the students were there when a stranger, a man, arrived with a small clock that he placed on a shelf to one side, where he could see it and Carol could not. He took a seat. All eyes looked expectantly at him, and he looked back at them, unsmiling and silent.

Debbie giggled, and said

"What happens now?" to the man, who shrugged his shoulders and looked around the group circle.

Carol had been anxious before he arrived, but now she could feel her heart racing. Two students came into the room with a cheery "Hi", which froze in the air as they took the last two vacant seats. One of them said she hadn't realized the time, and commented upon how quickly the group followed on from the teaching session with hardly any time to get a drink. Others agreed, and then the group fell silent. Then a large, flamboyantly dressed woman said that she had been in a PD group before and maybe they should agree some ground rules. Carol noticed that both she and Debbie looked at the facilitator to check his response.

There was one male student in the group, who had been quite vocal in the earlier part of the day. He had mentioned already that he "came from a business background" and Carol experienced him as very confident and articulate. He spoke directly to the facilitator.

"I would like to be clear of your role here. Are you a silent observer or do you contribute to the group? Can we expect any guidance from you in how to proceed, or will this be an exercise where the group have to discover the answers for themselves?"

Carol's stomach clenched.

The facilitator replied directly to him.

"You would like to take control of the group, I see."

This boat has been launched in turbulent waters. Amongst the waves, conflict and challenge are clearly visible. Power, authority and gender are dark shapes in the water. Not for them the cautious, calm beginning, establishing ground rules about how to behave. This group has started with emotion. The challenge is to be able to use the powerful feelings in order to learn, rather than to just experience them. If the first group is sitting cautiously in the boat at anchor, whilst discussing the circumstances under which it might be possible to cast off, this group has been launched down a steep ramp straight into the North Sea. Now the members have to grab hold of their oars and try to row.

The facilitator's style

The major difference in the two vignettes involves the style of facilitation. Of course, they are both caricatures, drawn for this purpose to highlight difference. In real life, experienced facilitators are rarely one dimensional, and have developed their own style, integrating elements of various models. Inexperienced facilitators may hold more tightly to what they perceive as their "model", to guide them through what can be a challenging journey.

As a member of either group, there is a lot to learn from these beginnings. In one example, it is clear that the facilitator is taking responsibility for certain boundaries in setting out the chairs and bringing a clock. There is a clear message that time matters. If you are this group, you should realize quickly that lateness will be perceived as a challenge, whether or not you feel it is at this stage. In the other example, it does not appear particularly important. The message in the other group seems to be that turning up late is acceptable behaviour. Maybe later on this will become an issue, but not yet.

In one example, the facilitator works hard to bring everyone into the group, suggests what the group might do, and is friendly and self-disclosing. There is a sense that the facilitator is looking after the group and its members. Apart from setting out the chairs, the members might feel that they have to make little effort. The facilitator will take care of things and they can cruise along comfortably. It is interesting though, that Carol finds herself wanting to take care of the facilitator. This may indicate that the issues of vulnerability and nurturing are already making their presence felt at a deeper level.

In the other group, the facilitator is clearly not in the business of looking after people, or wanting people to like him. His opening comment is a direct challenge to one member's intervention and in all likelihood will provoke a howl of protest, spoken or silent. Group members can be linked together in many ways—being angry with the facilitator is one of them.

There is an argument that exposing the group to strong emotion disturbs the ways in which we normally protect ourselves from each other, or the ways in which we defend against genuine contact. It puts down a challenge to communicate directly and with emotion, which after all, is a necessary condition for development to take place in the group. This style of beginning also makes clear that the group are going to have to do the work themselves. There is little chance of being gently led by the hand into self-discovery in this group.

Both styles that feature in the vignettes have their strong and weak points. Personally I think there is a valuable middle ground between nurturing and challenging, which respects the need to develop group relationships before tackling the powerfully emotive issues. However, as a group member, you will have to learn to make the best of whatever sort of facilitator you have in your PD group, as long as she or he does not behave in any unethical way. Groups of students have been known to refuse to work with facilitators, but it is rare and distressing occurrence and not one to rely upon to solve any difficulties with the facilitator

Think again about your first group meeting and focus now upon your reaction to the facilitator. In this exercise, the task is let yourself respond spontaneously, imaginatively, ridiculously - as uninhibitedly as you can. It is a type of exercise you will come across frequently in the book, and particularly valuable for discovering parts of yourself that might not always be easily accessible. It comes easier for some people than others, but can be developed with practice and will be enormously useful as a counsellor or therapist.

The first question to hold in mind is—"How would I describe the facilitator?" Write a list of words without pausing to think too much about any of them.

Move on to the next question, which is "Who does the facilitator remind me of?" Again, try and write "off the top of your head" rather than the bottom! Otherwise you might be tempted not to write everything down, but censor what you feel are inappropriate responses.

These first questions are trying to uncover associations and attitudes that may not all be obvious to you. The following questions are more in the style of detective work, sifting through the evidence of the first group meeting.

Do you remember anything that the facilitator said?

Do any particular moments stand out? If so, what was happening at this point? Why might it be significant for you?

Can you identify any emotional responses to the facilitator?

This last question should connect up with some of the replies to the first associative type questions, and help you to see something of the shape of your initial relationship with the group facilitator.

The two vignettes are in some ways very different beginnings, and much of that difference can be attributed to the style of facilitation and the type of course. But there are some fundamental aspects that the groups have in common, which in the longer term may prove more significant than the differences.

How to behave

Every group has to decide at some stage what is acceptable behaviour. In the examples above, the first group began at the outset to try to define norms of behaviour. This PD group was especially concerned with the expression of anger, which for many students is a key anxiety. There is a pervasive image in our culture that a therapy/encounter/PD group will be full of verbal attacks and dis-inhibited behaviour—as if "being authentic" equals "being aggressive". There is also the image of "mob rule", where group pressure turns perfectly reasonable people into savages, so it is not surprising that PD groups often wish to control the expression of anger.

The balance is important. If it is controlled too tightly, then no one may be able to raise their voice without being accused of breaking the rules. If it is not defined at all, then at some point the group may have to deal with a situation in which one member feels that another has been abusive, under the guise of being honest or congruent. There is a continual tension between the expectation to speak one's mind, and the awareness that this can legitimate verbal abuse. In addition, some accommodation has to be found between the desire to keep everything safe and comfortable, and the awareness that if no strong emotions are allowed into the group then very little learning is going to take place.

Some groups go on to develop more detailed norms of behaviour. Arriving on time, giving apologies for absences, and switching mobile phones off are all common and sensible examples of behaviour that group members commit themselves too. As in all democracies, it can take a long time to negotiate settlements between the laissez- faire faction, and the precautionary faction. Those who just want to see what happens may be exasperated by the legalistic and cautious approach of those who need to get everything clear before the ship is allowed to leave the dock.

Whatever the starting point, every group has to tackle the issue of acceptable behaviour at some point. The discussions do not necessarily lead to definite conclusions that can be written down as a constitution. The majority of groups arrive at a less clearly defined agreement, which is revised and restated again at various points in the journey. The important element is the process of talking and thinking about the issues as a group, which means every member picking up their oar and taking their part in shaping the nature of the group.

Confidentiality

This is another prime concern for the PD group that may initially appear straight forward, but in time reveals its complexity. Everyone is quite happy to agree that the group should be confidential, and then in the next meeting someone lets slip that they have been talking about the group with their partner.

"Did you just say you were talking about the group? But we agreed that it was confidential!"

"But I didn't think partners counted!"

"Well how do I know that your partner isn't going off to work and telling all his mates about something that you told him about the group?"

"I'm sure he'd never do that!"

"You might be sure—but it doesn't reassure me. I thought we'd agreed that whatever went on in the group stayed in the group."

"I'd not thought about it before, but I think Debbie's right. I wouldn't feel safe to say anything really personal in here if I thought it got discussed when people got home."

"Well, I tell my husband everything, I always have. We don't have any secrets between us and we never have. And I'm certainly not going to stop telling him things now!"

Absolute confidentiality is probably a myth, and if the boat can only set sail in these conditions it will not get very far. The group would do well to recognise this and negotiate a formula that allows for some degree of flexibility. A common agreement, for example, is that group members are free to talk about their own issues to whomever they like, but should take care not to mention other group members in this, or to discuss other member's business. Gossiping is a human characteristic and considerable self-discipline is required to maintain these boundaries. It is likely to break down for most students at some point during their time in the PD group. Instead of either denying this or berating oneself, it is more useful to reflect upon how and why it happened. In this way it can become a valuable piece of self-understanding and a good preparation for the boundary-keeping demands of counselling and therapy.

The boundary between PD group and the course in general is another area that raises concerns about confidentiality, unless some very clear guidelines have already been set down. The role played by the PD group in assessing a student's suitability to become a counsellor or therapist may be clear before the group begins. Often, however, this is not the case, and there is a reluctance to leave the quayside before establishing the manner in which information might be passed from the group to those assessing performance.

Physical environment

Every group has a physical environment that is set in a wider context. College, university, training institute, hired rooms—a range of different locations. At this initial stage it may not seem important, but in fact, the environment will play an important part in the life of the group.

Atmosphere permeates the workings of groups. A room that is gloomy and untidy sends unspoken messages of neglect and lack of importance that will permeate the workings of the group. These themes will resonate with those group members who bring into the group similar experiences of neglect, who feel themselves to be disregarded and undervalued, with no power to improve their situation.

The group may meet in the room where the teaching takes place. The atmosphere here is full of the teaching material and the interactions of the day, making it more difficult to create a separate psychological space for the work of the group.

Even more problematic is the lack of a consistent meeting place. Groups can be moved from room to room to accommodate other aspects of the timetable or other courses in the same building. Whatever the rhetoric, the message here is clearly that the group is not valued. Any group will struggle to work effectively if it cannot be found a consistent place in which to meet. PD groups need to be held in genuine positive regard within any course structure or institution, and this needs to be demonstrated in the environmental provision.

Connections and containers

In any group, there is a network of connections that hold members together. Like a web or mesh, members are joined with multiple strands to each other. One of the first challenges for the PD group is to establish this web of connectivity. This forms the "container" in which all the thoughts, emotions, relived experiences, fantasies and inter-relationships of the group members can be held and worked with. Obviously, nothing can be contained without a container; similarly, the more resilient the container, the more material it can handle.

The web is built up from the strands that link its members. In the examples, Debbie and Carol have formed some sort of link with each other that they bring into the PD group. Something attracted them to each other in the very earliest moments of meeting. We all make judgments about other people the moment that we see or hear them. Within the first few minutes we will have sensed whether or not we might like someone, and this usually relates to whether we perceive them as "like me" or "not like me". Much of this scanning goes on behind the scenes, out of our awareness. Physical characteristics, facial expressions, body language, dress, tone of voice—these are all types of evidence that we gather to ascertain the level of threat or promise posed by the stranger.

Draw a circle that represents your PD group, marking the names of all the members and the facilitator. Think about your own sense of affinity—who do you feel comfortable with? Who do you like, or think you might like at this point?

Draw a line from your own position in the circle across to a person who you feel positive about. Repeat this until you have exhausted all your positive links. Then, in a different colour, draw in the negative links, so that in your diagram there are a number of different coloured lines radiating out from your place in the circle which connect you to certain other members.

You may have drawn lots of lines or very few. What matters is becoming aware of your own affinities and the sorts of early connections that are forming in the PD group. If you imagine putting together the diagrams of all the members, then it is easy to recognise the "web" that is developing.

Prior connections

Carol and Debbie have already gone through this scanning process, as will have the other students, and all these connections are present from the very first group. There may be other significant links that have a longer history. Colleagues from the same workplace, students from the same introductory course, members of the same club, may find themselves on the same course and in the same PD group.

This can be a mixed blessing for both the individuals involved and for the PD group itself. Sharing the experience of a new course with someone that you already know can, on the plus side, provide a sense of security, companionship, and encouragement. The negative side is that it can be far more difficult to be open and direct with the person who gives you a lift home, or who you see next day at work. The relationship that exists outside of the boundaries of the course can inhibit the relationship within. Important things may not get said and worked with in the PD group for fear of damaging the relationship outside. The consequences may be a disappointing lack of movement in terms of personal growth for the individuals concerned, and a "no-go" area within the group communications network.

It is an uncomfortable position both for the individuals and for the group if this happens. The group requires a level of openness and directness if it is to become effective, and censorship restricts its possibilities. The more issues that are kept under wraps or taken outside of the group, the less adventurous the journey in the group is likely to be.

Themes and issues

Despite the difference in the initial meeting, these two groups are heading in a similar direction. They each have a male facilitator and one male group member, and it is apparent from the outset that, in both examples, there is a tension between the two. Gender is a powerful element in any group, and in these two groups it is on the agenda right from the start.

Power and authority are entwined with gender. Where does the authority lie in the group? Who has the power to determine what happens? Who will be a leader and who a follower? There is a challenge in each group, more explicit in one than the other but nonetheless present in both. Questions of power might be difficult to talk about, especially in the early stages of a group, but they are always ticking away in the background. There will be work to be done in both groups around this issue.

Another theme right from the start concerns boundaries. From the very first session, members are coming in late, and it is highly likely that this will be addressed at some point. Every type of behaviour sends a message and the group will need to decode these types of messages if it is to develop an open network of communication.

Perhaps it was anxiety that made it hard for the latecomers to be there on time. Perhaps they do not believe that their presence matters. Perhaps they habitually turn up late—why would that be? There are layers of understanding that can be made available to the group and its members. It involves a lot of hard work on everybody's part, but the rewards are an effective PD group.

The very first group session is bursting with clues and information that every member can use if they actively reflect upon what happened. Trying to both identify themes and then relate them to personal experience is one of the important skills to develop during the journey. Using the boat metaphor, this is the first step in learning to row.

CHAPTER FOUR

Learning to row

If the PD group is a boat, it needs a set of oars and a crew to get it moving. Learning how to catch the wind or the tides comes with experience, and if the crew has amongst it members someone who has been here before and learnt some of the skills, that can be very helpful. Often, though, it is a crew of "beginners" who have clambered on board and have to try and get this boat out of the harbour and into the sea. At this stage, it is important to know something about how to row.

Some students fling themselves into the boat and grab an oar, enthusiastically. They are keen to get going, to see where this journey will take them, and however inexpertly set about the task of getting the boat moving. Others sit cautiously, eyeing up the situation and wondering if and when to begin. For some group members, there is a strong resistance to joining in. They fold their arms and transmit the message "Don't expect me to pick up an oar."

But suppose for now that this is boat full of enthusiastic would-be sailors, keen to travel to distant shores. In a real boat, it would be reasonable to expect some instruction, and many PD groups begin from this point. The sensible approach would be to ask, "How do we do this?"

The group may wrestle with this question and come up with some answers. They may agree, for example, that members will speak for themselves using "I", rather than a generalised "we". There may also be a clear expectation that the conversation in the group will focus upon the "here and now". Talking about things that go on outside of the group may be deemed inappropriate in this setting. Other groups may operate with a different remit that gives permission to talk about "everything". These broad guidelines based on content may not get the group very far, however.

In practise, the significant conversations are likely to be very similar whatever the group expectations. The "here-and-now" group will find itself at times engaged in painful material about past events triggered by a present situation. The "talk about everything" group will be challenged to engage in conversations that are of real significance, which will include here- and- now interactions as well as past events. It is not possible to rinse the present free of the past, and this inter-relationship is something to be explored in every group.

This leaves the group in the position of still searching for answers to the question of how to proceed. One thing is quite certain, and that is the need to work together. The boat needs the best efforts of all of the crew. One person rowing like mad will not produce an epic journey.

Structure

In almost every PD group there will be an attempt to solve the problems of communication and relationship by structure. The great thing about structure is that it imposes control and order on a potentially chaotic situation. Clear expectations and clear guidelines relieve the anxiety, give purpose to the enterprise and enable to boat to set sail. Everyone agrees on a formula that provides instructions on how to row, so that the boat can get going on its journey.

The most common suggestion involves creating an allotted time span for every member to speak, sometimes called a "check in" or "checkout" if it is designed as an introductory or concluding structure. In this way, the argument runs, everyone has an equal share of the time and is expected to contribute equally. Every voice will have its allocated opportunity to be heard.

Other common structures rely upon topics—"let's choose a different subject to talk about each week", or exercises—"I've got this book with some really great group exercises we could do" or asking the facilitator—"you're the expert, you tell us how to do this".

In some groups, structure does play a useful part in the initial stages. It lowers anxiety, and enables the boat to set off. Unfortunately, it may then be restricted to sailing around a pond, because structure also provides constraints. Certain conversations cannot be had because there is no space within the turn-taking formula, for example. Interesting comments are made but the structure does not allow enough time for them to be followed through.

Group exercises have a dual function of bringing something into the group but keeping other, usually more problematic things out. They can restrict growth in a similar way to turn taking. The third option of allowing or forcing the facilitator to control the agenda will seriously limit the potential for adult growth. Group members have to take up their own responsibility for the nature of their group if they are to psychologically develop. For all these reasons, most groups will decide at some point that the price for lowering anxiety through structure is too high.

The other reason for jettisoning the structured approach is that there are usually some dissenting voices of members who do not wish to be controlled by whichever structure is being proposed. Where this happens, there is no casting off under the protection of a regulatory structure. The group can only move as the members learn to row. The challenge of communicating with each other has to be engaged with from the outset.

Making links

Group members need each other if they are to learn anything from the PD group experience. They need to get to know each other and to build relationships.

Holding this firmly in mind, each member can begin to search for someone they are able to work with. Right from the outset, members will have intuitively identified the others with whom they feel some affinity. These initial links can be used productively in the early sessions to build and strengthen the web of connections that will form the basis for the group's journey.

Imagine a situation in a group where one member, Farida, says, "I hate it when nobody speaks". Across the circle, Ann thinks, "So do I", but says nothing. The facilitator might inquire if anyone shares Farida's feeling about silences. Ann knows that she does, but says nothing. The outcome of these few minutes is minimal, and possibly negative. Farida perhaps feels that she wishes she had kept her mouth shut and feels rejected by the lack of response.

There is another possible outcome.

Farida: I hate it when nobody speaks.
Ann: So do I. It makes me feel anxious.
Farida: I try really hard to think of something to say but then my mind is a complete blank.
Ann: Yes, me too. But it seems such a waste of time if we just all sit here and say nothing.
Farida: I hate doing nothing. It's just not like me. I'm usually always busy, busy, busy. Then we come in here and just sit, and I can feel myself getting more and more agitated.
Darren: It doesn't bother me. I can just think about things in my head— it feels like a break to me, nobody going on about anything. Sort of peaceful.
Ann: But is that what we're supposed to be doing here? Having a break?

Now three group members are getting involved in a conversation about how to work in the group—and all because Ann picked up her oar and started to row with Farida. If they continued the conversation, they might begin to discover that they had other things in common apart from their discomfort with silence and not being busy. They might, if more members pick up their own oars, find that other members have similar or different attitudes. From here, they might get to a place where they start to wonder what it is that makes them react in a particular way to the silence in the group. And once they reach this point, they can potentially learn something about themselves.

The message here is clear. A response can push the boat along, like an oar dipping in the water. It may be a shallow stroke, but it creates movement. Ann and Farida are cautiously dipping their oars into the water, offering each other some mutual encouragement, and then another member joins in. In this way, momentum can gather, and the boat moves off.

The web of connections needs knitting together in the early days of the group. Intuitive links can be reinforced by conscious efforts to "row together" where group members work to identify points of similarity or difference.

Fog

Many students have the experience of sitting in the group circle, unable to "think of anything to say", just like Farida in the example. Fog invades the brain and it feels as if there is nothing else there— a grey blanket covering the internal landscape. As far as the students are aware, they are trying hard to find ways of participating and are frustrated by their own blankness. Out of their awareness, they are wrapping themselves in the grey blanket for protection.

Speaking openly in the group might generate an unexpected, perhaps hostile, response. Where would it lead? Once the words are out, there is no control over the outcome—anything could happen. The anxious, self protecting parts of each of us can move into action behind the scenes to prevent us from setting off on this potentially exposing and dangerous path. Fog is one of the first weapons to be brought into action.

It is helpful to recognise that the fog has a clear purpose. It has been created to prevent communication, and evaporates once it fails in its mission. In the example, Farida puts the feeling into words rather than let it silence her, which is a productive technique in the struggle to throw off the grey blanket. Once a student becomes suspicious of the fog, then they have begun to resist it.

They may well discover, if they pay close attention to what is happening in these foggy times, that there are discernible shapes in the landscape after all. Rather than being unable to think of anything to say, the internal dialogue is dominated by censorship. Various topics are suggested, only to be rejected as too risky, or too trivial. The internal censor judges that all the ideas are inappropriate in one way or another, so that nothing can be said.

This sort of self-reflection will prove helpful in dealing with the grey blanket, but it needs to be supported by muscle power. It is easy to wrap the blanket around oneself, because, like most blankets, it offers an element of comfort. It is a struggle to push it away, requiring real effort and determination.

If you recognise these experiences, fight back with some reflective exercises. These can be done both in retrospect, looking back on the experience after the group meeting, or in real time, as it is happening. Recovering the ability to think about what is happening is the first step in dispersing the fog.

What was happening in the group when you felt unable to think of anything? Can you recall the detail—who was sitting where, what had been discussed, what the group went on to deal with?

Pay close attention to your own feelings. What were the emotions that accompanied "not being able to think of anything"?

Now survey again your thought processes. What was happening beneath the fog? Were there ideas that you thought of and then rejected?

What were they? Why were they rejected?

Responding

One of the most important ways in which communication within the PD group differs from that of other social groups is the degree of openness and transparency. This does not often require any skill or expertise other than the willingness to say aloud what is being thought. On one level, it is surprisingly simple, but it is likely to take some time to learn how to do this.

It involves un-learning many of the social rules of conversation that protect us from both intimacy and aggression. We disguise our emotions, agree when we have differing opinions, smile when we feel angry or afraid, keep silent rather than risk conflict, protect our privacy—an extensive interlocking range of social conventions which enable us to co-exist in superficial harmony. Even in our closer relationships, the risks of exposing what we feel or what we think can seem too great. It is not therefore surprising that communicating openly can be such a challenge.

Each culture has its own set of norms defining what may and may not be said, in which particular contexts, and to whom. Within the culture there will be variations according to gender, class, age, status and other sub-groupings. Particular topics may be labelled taboo—such as death, religion, sex, and incest.

The PD group has the task of defining its own norms of communication. One example of this is the attempt to draw up the ground rules that was discussed earlier. The more subtle aspects of responding and initiating are too complex to regulate in any formulaic system, and the group will have to construct them as it develops. The group itself is embedded within a system of powerful pre-existing norms that largely go un-noticed, and each member has been programmed according to their particular culture and family experience to communicate in certain ways.

Recognising and letting go of aspects of this cultural programming—whatever the culture—can feel simultaneously liberating and frightening. Some of these conventions have arisen through time for some very sound reasons. Without them, there is a real fear of both of being attacked, and attacking. We do not always say what we think or feel because we fear the consequences—hurting others or being hurt ourselves through retaliation. Achieving some sense of balance between sensitivity to others and faithfulness to one's own experience does not come without a lot of hard work. Risks have to be taken and mistakes will inevitably be made. Practising in shallow water seems a sensible idea.

In the PD group there is a silence, broken by Cara, a woman who dresses neatly, speaks very precisely and sits very still. She finishes every statement with a brief smile. Suzi is a large woman whose contributions so far have always been expressions of concern, care, and empathy. Ann wears light sensitive glasses, which means that under the artificial light in the room, she looks as if she is wearing sunglasses. Darren fidgets a lot and always sits next to the male facilitator.

Cara: *I need to tell the group that I won't be here next week because I have to go to a funeral.*
Suzi: *I'm sorry you won't be here—funerals can be horrible*
Cara: *It's my stepmother. We were never close, so I don't expect it will be too emotional. And it will be a chance to see my half sister again—we don't meet up very often.*
(Brief silence)

Ann: My stepmother died two years ago. I was very fond of her, and I still miss her.

Caroline: That sounds very different from my experience. My sister got on better with her than I did, but she never liked me. I think I got in the way, and came between her and my father too much. I left home when I was 17 and I can still remember how relieved I—

Darren: I left home at 17, too.

This brief vignette provides an example of possible ways in which to respond. There are a variety of levels and possible connections at each level. The most apparent is "content"—what it is that is being discussed. The spoken material has a number of themes that can be gathered under the following headings—step-parenting, and by implication, parenting; siblings; funerals and by implication, death; loss; leaving home. There are going to be very few members of the group who do not have any experience of any of these topics. All of them provide a way in to a conversation that will enable group members to get to know each other better. For example—

"I always felt that my sister had a much better relationship with my mother than I did—like you said, Cara. She was the favourite one, and I felt very left out as a child" said Patti.

Non-verbal communication offers another possible way of developing connections. Cara's smile, Anne's lack of eye contact, Darren's fidgeting—these are all communications that provoke responses.

"It's hard for me to see your eyes, Anne, in your dark glasses. It makes me feel cut off from you—maybe a bit threatened, too," said Jonathan.

The response here is a comment upon something that the whole group will be aware of, and an acknowledgment of its personal impact. Group sessions are full of non-verbal communications that need to be talked about and thought about it their meaning is to become clear. Learning to row involves taking the risk of putting into words what you see, and how you feel about what you see.

"Process" is a concept that will appear again and again here. Instead of focussing upon what is being said or communicated, a process level connection would address how the group is communicating. Noticing how the group operates, recognising repeating patterns, and exploring these aspects are all very productive forms of rowing, which can move the boat along in the water at high speed.

In the vignette, three particular aspects of process stand out—Darren's interruption, his consistent choice of seat, and Suzi's pattern of "caring" interventions. All will generate a response somewhere in the group.

"*You always sit next to the facilitator, Darren. I was thinking about that when you were speaking, and I wondered why you always did that. I realised that I would never choose to sit there myself!*" said Patti.

Again, verbalising both what is noticed and some personal impact invites the other group member to respond whilst owning that there are perhaps interesting things to be learnt from all sides.

Initiating

Initiating and responding are of course intimately bound up with each other and often indistinguishable. Every response initiates something; every initiative is a response to something else. But in the context of learning to row, it is a justifiable to make a distinction between the two. In these terms, the member of a new group who says "There's something I want to talk about" is initiating a conversation.

Think about your last PD group meeting. Choose a period of time when there was a dialogue and write down, as accurately as you can, what went on for several minutes. It does not need to be a very long vignette.

Write down ways in which the group material connected with your own experience.
    Use the three headings of—

- Content
- Non verbal communication
- Process

Having written it, look at all the possible ways that you might have responded.

It is impossible to build healthy relationships without at times taking the initiative, and at times being the listener and the respondent. Building a positive relationship with the group, as well as the members, involves exactly the same balance. Some students may rely upon picking up their oar only in response to another member's contribution. As the group will need all its members to be able to row on their own initiative, these students may benefit from practice on dry land.

Nita feels stretched between family, work and the course. Her eldest daughter is very challenging and angry at home, and the youngest is suddenly refusing to go to school. Her divorced husband sees the girls very infrequently and offers little support She enjoys the course but finds the PD group a trial. She says very little, even when other group members encourage her to participate. Her best friend Rumi insists that they meet up for coffee at the weekend, and Nita is telling her about the PD group.

Nita: I know what you're going to say—if I don't put anything in, I won't get anything out. I know that.

Rumi: There's so much going on in your life right now, Nita—you could do with some space to talk about things. Does the group know about the girls?

Nita: No, sometimes I think I might say something but then the moment passes and somebody's talking about something else. Nobody seems to have any problems with their children.

Rumi: Oh come off it—everyone has problems with their kids at some point. There's bound to be some other mum struggling in the group.

Nita: Well, she's keeping quiet then, like me!

Rumi: Are you frightened that they'll all think you're pathetic or something?

Nita: How can I be a good counsellor if I can't even sort out my own problems? That's what everyone will think—won't they?

Rumi: If you're going to learn anything about yourself in this group you've got to get past this one, Nita. Everyone thinks that at some time or another—you'll see.

This dialogue reveals that not only does Nita have a pre-occupying concern that she is not sharing in the group, but also the source of her reluctance to use the group. Anticipating judgments and negative reactions is one of the most common reasons for sitting back and not taking the initiative.

The key questions are "How could the group get to know me better? What would they need to know about me? What is important to me?" It will be difficult to get to know Nita without appreciating her current preoccupation with the relationship with her daughters. Similarly, she will not feel that she is understood or heard unless this difficulty is brought into the group container. Even for those students who feel that their lives are unremarkable, with no particular difficulties or problems, these questions are valid.

How would anyone get to know you? What would they need to know? What are the things that are important to you?

Are there things that you know are important but you are reluctant to share? What do you fear?

Make a list of all the things that you would share in a close relationship. Choose one and imagine how you might share it in your group. What words would you use? What reaction would you anticipate?

Disclosure

When tragedies and traumas are shared, there is the possibility of both intimacy and healing. At some point in the life of the PD group, members are very likely to share some painful and distressing experiences with each other. There is a very positive deepening of relationships that can come out of these disclosures, and they can enrich the life of the community that is the group.

There are, however, some negative outcomes where members feel over exposed, too vulnerable, not heard, or ashamed. There are many variables in this, but timing can be highly significant. PD groups have the capacity to contain and work with very painful and distressing emotions, but they need time to build up their resources. The web of inter-relationships needs to be in place, like a safety net, to catch hold of the group member who dives from the topmast into the boat. Many people intuitively know this, and hold on to their stories until the group feels more secure. But others, whose relationships have been very damaging or abusive, can find it difficult to judge when to jump in. Disclosing powerful material in the very early sessions of group life can sometimes lead to powerful feelings of shame, or anger at the response. The member may leave prematurely, or may never recover enough to use the group productively.

Disclosure can be elevated as the key task for the student in the PD group, putting pressure upon members to "tell all". It is more helpful to view it as one of the many possible ways to communicate, which needs a responsive context if it is to have to have a creative outcome. This outcome also assumes that the member who discloses is able to hear and make use of the responses, even if they are unexpected or unwelcome. Members disclose for different reasons, not all of them out of an authentic desire to learn something about themselves.

At this point, the fiction of assuming that all members are eager to row and learn more about themselves becomes difficult to sustain. People behave in complex ways, some of which they are aware of and others less so. Recognising ambivalence and resistance are very useful if the boat is to travel far at all.

CHAPTER FIVE

Undercurrents

Despite all efforts, it may seem that the boat resolutely refuses to move out of the harbour. It is trapped, floating up and down the same stretch of water and unable to find a passage through to the open sea.

This sense of immobility is a recurring sensation in groups, and with time can be understood as a prelude to change; a necessary gathering of energy in order to unfurl a sail, perhaps, or an indication of some resistance to travelling further that needs understanding in the group. In the early stages of a PD group however, it can seem as if the boat will never ever get going. This chapter looks at some of those elements that might be making movement difficult.

Resistance

The group may discover that not every member is willing to take up their oar and row. This can be explicitly and openly acknowledged, or gradually become apparent.

The resistance might focus upon either "personal development" or "group" or both.

There are students whose superficial openness to personal development evaporates rapidly once they have gained a place on the course. Some students pay little attention to the personal development aspects of training other than pragmatically acknowledging their importance at interview. Certain trainings are more prestigious and difficult to get into than others, and the prospective candidate needs to be enthusiastic about all the elements. Whether or not this genuinely matches with her or his personal attitude is revealed at a later date.

"Really I don't see why we need to spend all this time looking into ourselves when it's the clients that we need to understand. It's just self indulgent and a waste of time as far as I'm concerned".

Therapy as a relational experience is thrown overboard in favour of a clear patient/therapist divide. The patient/client has the problems and the therapist/expert is required to solve them. It is such a familiar and apparently sensible way of thinking about psychological problems because it replicates the dominant attitude to physical problems in our culture. We have a pain, so we go to the doctor/expert who clarifies the nature of the problem and prescribes a solution.

The role of the therapist as "expert" is rejected in many training models, but is certainly not dead in the water. Within the context of the health service in particular, the majority of client/patients will initially assume that the counsellor or therapist is an expert. Even though they may come to take a different view, the assumption from the outset is that they are talking with an expert of some sort. Why go and talk with a stranger who is not an expert? Inside the world of counselling there are some clear answers to this question, but outside it may seem unanswerable and ridiculous. Trainees come from "outside" and many bring with them these culturally dominant attitudes which value expertise rather than relationship.

Trainings themselves have differing attitudes to the relative importance of "relational encounter" and "expertise". Some clinical psychology trainings, for example, clearly emphasize knowledge, skills and expertise, whilst others encourage the development of the "self-reflexive practitioner". The expert and the self-reflexive practitioner co-exist and at times conflict within the professional group. This is echoed within the trainee group, finding its way inevitably into the PD group.

Other models and trainings struggle less obviously but significantly with the relationship between "encounter" and "expertise" so it is no surprise to find this conflict or ambivalence present in a range of PD groups. If the underlying commitment to personal development is absent or at least uncertain, then the group is confronted with a reluctant crewmember or members right from the start.

This is not the only ground for refusing to row. Even if the idea of personal development is genuinely valued, there is another common resistance, which uses the fact of "group" to justify sitting back and letting the others get on with it. (Chapter 1)

"To be honest, I've always hated groups and I don't see any value in this experience for me. It's fine for some people I'm sure, but not for me and I'm going to do my own personal developing in other ways—in individual therapy and in supervision".

Many in the group will be frustrated by this attitude, thinking quite reasonably that anyone who hated groups should not have chosen to come on a course where there was a PD group. However, people choose courses for many reasons—location, accessibility, cost, theoretical orientation, timing, to name some examples. In the overall scheme, the PD group may have seemed a minus point outweighed by other positive factors. But now it becomes a reality and has to be responded to. Fortunately, the initial stance that a member takes is not always the one that prevails as the reality takes hold. The group's capacity to acknowledge and work with the strong feelings that are generated by a clear refusal to row will be a significant factor.

These are examples of open resistance that the group will have to struggle with. It is tempting to think that if only these reluctant members could be persuaded to join in and row, or to leave the course, that the boat could then cut through the waves at great speed. The reality is likely to be that these clear voices of resistance drown out the quieter, more mumbled tones of resistance within all the group members. The polarization of attitudes into the pro- and anti-PD group disguises the ambivalence within the group as a whole.

Ambivalence

Emotions, like tides, wax and wane. Sometimes the waves lap against the sea wall, covering the beach, and at other times withdraw far out to sea, hardly visible on the horizon. Enthusiasm and hopefulness can withdraw to reveal negativity and passivity.

When the tide is neither in nor out, we can be aware of experiencing conflicting sets of emotions and thoughts.

Initial enthusiasm gives way to a sinking recognition of the efforts and exertions required. At this point it is easier to recognise our own mixed feelings about this PD group experience. Even the most enthusiastic student is going to feel at times frustrated, angry, impotent, upset, and destabilised—and this is in a group that is working well.

Rhian had wondered about saying anything in the group when she heard Linda talking about drug addiction. Linda seemed to have some very definite opinions about the sort of people who took drugs, and Rhian had wondered if she worked with addiction in some way. But Tom had asked the same question and it turned out that Linda's opinions were based on things she heard or read in the media. Tom had gently challenged Linda on this, and she had light heartedly admitted that yes, it wasn't perhaps the best source of information.

The whole exchange could only have taken up five minutes of group time, but Rhian was very pre-occupied, and irritated with Linda. She sat in silence for the rest of the session, and when someone asked her about this, she brushed it off by saying she had a headache.

Rhian is struggling with an internal conflict. Up until this point she has been an active member of the group, trying out her rowing skills with enthusiasm. Now she is faced with a problematic choice, and she is ambivalent. She can pretend that nothing significant has happened, or she can acknowledge that she had some strong feelings in the group and look at what might be happening for her. This is what she wrote in her own learning journal.

"I felt really angry with L. making her smug judgments about the sort of families that drug addicts come from. I know I should tell her—that's the whole point of this group and just what I was saying the week before last. All this stuff about being open and honest with each other that I was going on about. But the moment I tell her then someone will ask why it upset me so much—so obvious of course, and then I have to tell them about my little brother and his cocaine problems—I would feel so bad, like betraying him and the family. I would have to talk about how I feel about the whole terrible mess—I don't know how I feel, it's all a muddle. Angry, very angry, yes— and so sad, desperately sad. It's like pulling a thread—once I say anything about this in the group, it will lead onto more and more, and do I really want that? But if I keep it all out of the group then I'm not being this open person who can learn about herself—and part of me wants that as well. Help!"

Ambivalence is uncomfortable and sometimes difficult to hold onto. It is usually tempting to get rid of the discomfort by pushing one side of the argument out of the way. In a group setting, this discomfort is often solved by sharing out the opposing views between members. Up to this point, Rhian was in the "yes, let's row" party, whilst another member was firmly in the "not me" category. Now Rhian has to face up to the realization that she too has an internal reluctant rower.

Recognising the other in oneself is such an important part of personal development. At first it is difficult to see that the things that bother us about other people are generally the things that we ourselves struggle with. As the group progresses, more and more of these moments of recognition will illuminate the journey. Within the network of communication in a group, these moments are not just individual, personal revelations, but demonstrate the inter-relationships that characterize group process.

Rhian's recognition of her own ambivalence could be very instrumental in helping the other member to recognize that she too has

---

Do this exercise when you are in a comfortable place with no threat of interruption.

Think about those things that you would never want to talk about in the PD group and write them down. Ask the following questions about each of the things that you have written down.

1. How do I imagine I would feel if I did talk about this in the group? Write down all the "feeling" words that come to mind.
2. What responses might I get? (This is as imaginative, not rational, exercise).
3. What would be the worst possible outcome?

Now put yourself in the position of hearing another group member talk about one of the things that is on your list.

1. How do you imagine you would feel?
2. What do you think would be the response of others in the group?

mixed feelings, and that part of her does want to share in the group journey. But for that to happen, Rhian needs to say something in the next PD group. Being able to openly talk about discovering her own resistance, and her reluctance to expose herself and her family, will move the boat along without necessarily focusing upon her brother.

Absence

One of the most obvious things that hold the group back from its journey is the shortage of rowers. Empty chairs in the group circle are always a problem. The group sets off in a certain direction one week but is unable to sustain the impetus because the next week, some people are missing and some who were absent return. The effect is to keep the boat tied up in the harbour, frustrating the keen rowers who want to travel serious distances.

Of course, absent members usually have good reasons why they cannot attend—someone has died, someone is ill, there is a family meal, the cat has to be taken to the vet, there is a parents evening or a school play, a partner's birthday and so on and so on. The other members might think that it would be unreasonable to get angry about the absences in these circumstances. These events happen in everyone's life, and who know when it might happen to oneself. So everyone politely accepts the explanation and the group struggles to get going again.

The group has met eight times, and there has never been an occasion when every member has been present. Millie and Sach have each missed 2 of the eight sessions, Cheryl, Paul and Permjit have missed one each, whilst Sandra, Daniela and Jean have attended every group. The facilitator has also been absent for one session through illness. There have been some interesting conversations in the group about vulnerability and self-protectiveness, and Jean in particular has been open about her own struggles in her relationship. Permjit and Millie have said very little, but all of the others seem prepared to tentatively take hold of an oar and dip it in the water. It seems to be a group that has a lot of potential, but is continually trying to "catch up" the members who have missed an important group event.

In the ninth session, Mille has sent her apologies, saying that her daughter is unwell, and Cheryl had to leave the course early for a dental appointment and so can't make the group.

Jean says, "I know they have to do these things, but I do find it frustrating" (What she actually thinks is "I am really pissed off with Millie. There is always some excuse why she can't be here. What's the point of being in a PD group and never attending!")

Sach says, "You can't drop everything for the group, can you? Life goes on and you have to sort things out. Millie can't help it if her daughter's ill, can she?" (What he thinks is—"Don't put pressure on absences because that will affect me".)

Jean says. "No, of course not". (What she thinks is "Bloody good excuse", and then feels guilty for the thought.)

Daniela says, "Cheryl told me that she did try to rearrange her appointment but wasn't able to." (What she thinks is "let's not get angry with anyone, let's just support each other. I hope Jean's not going to make a fuss." What she feels is anxiety.)

The group then get into a conversation about how hard it is to get dental appointments and the terrible state of dentistry in the UK.

Maybe the group is struggling to find its teeth. No one wants to rock the boat here, but under the surface there are some negative feelings that cannot yet be talked about. Absences communicate something—all behaviour is a form of communication, but at this stage it is not being said in words but actions. It is usually a relief when a group member says something like—

"Well, if I'm honest I didn't really feel that ill. I could have got to the group but I suppose I just decided, stuff it!"

Now the group can get its teeth into what is going on and talk to each other more openly. Often when this happens, other absenting members are able to own their own reluctance to be in the group. They too may be able to acknowledge that, at times, the very reasonable explanations were at least in part, excuses. Ambivalence, reluctance, and resistance can begin to be part of the group conversation rather than entangling the boat beneath the water and disabling it.

When the group is working well, absences cease to be problematic. The group are caught up in their own story and even when things are tough, members do not want to miss the next episode. If circumstances mean that they have to, there is genuine regret that the others can recognise and acknowledge. They know each other well enough to recognise their mutual commitment to the journey. Absences in this context are still interesting communications that the group will want to listen for, but they are not expressing resistance in the way that they can do in the earlier stages.

Lateness

Much of this also applies to lateness. Being late communicates something in actions rather than words, and whilst it is in this format the group and the individual miss an opportunity to learn something important. Sometimes what is revealed goes beyond resentment and ambivalence to touch on other areas of personal significance.

Charlene was always late for the PD group—not very late, just a few minutes, but never quite on time. She would sit quietly for the first ten minutes or so, and then gradually enter the group conversation, so that by the time the group ended, she was a very active member. This pattern would then repeat itself the following week. She appeared to be a strong character, with definite views and ideas. Perhaps this was why nobody asked her about the persistent lateness. Finally, the facilitator mentioned it.

Charlene's response was very defensive and the group got nowhere with the conversation.

The following group session, Charlene was again a few minutes late. The group was sitting quietly, as if waiting for her, but the silence continued after her arrival. A conversation started up and died. Then another, but it seemed as if the group were waiting to get started. The facilitator, Sue, asked what might be going on in the group. Lin said to her in a rather accusing voice that she was finding it difficult to concentrate. Since Sue had drawn attention to Charlene's lateness, she found herself very aware of it and did not know how to move on.

Another silence followed, broken to the group's relief by Charlene.

She had been very angry after the last group, she told them, and had let off steam to her partner. But her partner had said that it was quite right, she was always a few minutes late, and what's more, it was really annoying. This had made her think more about it and acknowledge that there was a pattern here.

Various group members were keen to play the part of detective and set about asking questions. It was not a productive move and Charlene seemed to become increasingly resistant to engage. Lin then said she thought maybe she had a similar problem, and talked about the times when she was feeling anxious and could never leave the house on time because she always had to check that she had everything she needed. This would mean that she was always in a rush, never leaving enough time to get to appointments and consequently arriving late.

Charlene had listened intently whilst Lin was talking. Being released from the hunt for clues was a relief, and she looked visibly more relaxed. She spoke again, saying that Lin's description had reminded her of something—she didn't know why because it was quite a different experience from the one that Lin had been talking about, but nevertheless, this incident from her childhood had come into her mind.

She was 7 or 8 years old and had changed schools. She felt like an outsider and was very unhappy there. Then another girl invited her to a birthday party. She was so excited, choosing the present, dressing up in her party frock—so much looking forward to this party. It was being held in the local parish hall and her big sister dropped her off there. A woman asked her what she was doing and she explained that she had come for the party.

"You're far too early. It doesn't start for ages yet. Can't you come back later?"

Charlene had shaken her head, so the woman had showed her into a huge empty room. "You'll just have to wait here then," she said and left.

As she described her feelings, standing for what felt like hours in a corner of this bare and empty room, Charlene's voice was full of emotion. When the birthday girl and her parents finally showed up, Charlene felt that she was a nuisance and in the way. All the excitement had turned into a terrible feeling in her stomach and the dream event had become a nightmare.

"But I can't see how that has anything to do with being late now—it was years and years ago. That's just too ridiculous," said Charlene.

Ridiculous or not, the childhood incident has appeared in the group for a reason, and the group now has the possibility of working to understand the links between past and present. For Charlene in particular, but also for Lin, the exploration for what lies beneath lateness can lead them into new personal insights. For the group, this move from passive acceptance to curiosity about meanings can open the harbour gates and give it greater possibilities for travel. Curiosity about what behaviour may communicate, and listening beyond the words, are key skills in counselling and psychotherapy that are often taught in the "advanced" stages. In the PD group, there is the opportunity to develop these skills right from the start.

There are many varied stories that lie behind lateness, and the task is to speak them and to hear them. Sometimes these stories have very individual meanings, as in Charlene's case. Often, they relate to the more general sense of reluctance that prevents a member from learning to row. Being late takes energy out of the group, slows it down, disrupts it, and can paralyse it. Why would any of these outcomes be desirable? Why should any group member want to sabotage the group journey?

Fear and anger

Whether the resistance comes in the form of a dramatic refusal to row or a more ambivalent will I/won't I, the underlying cause is very likely to be a sense of threat.

Groups provoke powerful emotions and for that reason can be feared. All of us are resistant to losing our securities and certainties about who we are. The PD group has to destabilise if it is to promote growth, and although intellectually we know this, it does not stop us putting up a powerful defence against it actually happening. Students can give themselves and others a variety of reasons why not to engage in the group, but the underlying reason is often fear.

Fear of being overwhelmed by emotion, fear of annihilation, fear of destructiveness, fear of difference and otherness, fear of meaninglessness—being alive involves a constant negotiation with fear and anxiety. Sometimes it can feel as if the hold we have on the positive aspects such as joy, love, and creativity, is too fragile to expose it to any destabilising experience. This can at times be openly acknowledged within the PD group—

"I don't want to talk about what's going on for me right now. I feel like I'm only just holding it together and if I talk about it I'll fall apart".

There are other familiar statements that justify keeping things exactly as they are—

"There are things going on for me that I need to sort out but it's not the right time to talk about them in the group."

"I'm a very private person and it takes a lot for me to share things with people"

"It won't make any difference if I talk about it—the problem will be just the same except that I'll feel worse. So let's leave it."

"I'm the sort of person who handles things on my own. I've always been like that"

All of these statements can be said in various tones—some of them timid and self-deprecating, others defiant and challenging.

The other side of fear is anger. These two powerful emotions are both responses to some sort of threat or danger and are versions of the instinctive "fight or flight" reaction. The group is perceived as a psychological threat that must be resisted, either actively or passively. It is the enemy and needs to be fought or fled from. This is acted out in the PD group by both withdrawal and attack.

Anger may be focussed upon the PDgroup-as-a-whole, particular people within it or those outside of the group—a different PD group, tutors, perhaps the course itself. Directing the anger outside of the group is a common occurrence in the early stages, before the group has learnt that this is usually relates to anger *within* the group.

Once anger can be openly expressed and talked about however, the group is on the move. Active, open anger may be uncomfortable, but it has an obvious life and energy that the group can engage with. It is these more passive versions, in the early stages, which can tie up the boat in a stranglehold of seaweed.

Most members will find themselves refusing to row, or resisting, at some point in the journey. Every member will feel sometimes that they don't want to be emotionally or intellectually disturbed. Things are fine as they are, don't rock the boat, let sleeping dogs lie, better the devil you know . . . and so on. It is not necessarily a permanent condition, but one that comes and goes until the member-group relationship grows into a less threatening configuration. As always, the task is to use the experience for learning more about the group and oneself.

This is a type of creative exercise, which requires an element of playfulness. The rational adult needs to move over and let some other part of you take charge here.

Imagine you are going on a sea journey but are not clear of the exact destination. You cannot quite remember why you signed up for this trip, but you have paid your money and there's no going back. At first it seems unfamiliar, but you are tied up in the harbour and the sea wall provides a sense of security. You have never been on an extended sea journey before and can only imagine what might lie ahead. The day of departure comes.

Now continue the story and complete these sentences.

The sky was ...., and the sea looked .... I went up on deck and stared at the horizon. My heart was .... I thought longingly of ....

It had been explained to us that we would have to row the boat out of the harbour, as this sort of boat did not have an engine. This had .... me.

It was .... as I had imagined.

I am a .... sort of person, and the thought of rowing was quite ....

We set off and it was .... than I thought. Looking ahead, I thought I could see .... The weather was changing and I looked over the side into the water. It was .... and..........................

I could see the harbour wall behind me now, and as the boat rose and fell with the waves, I thought "........................."

If you have been able to put yourself into it imaginatively, you might want to continue the story to see where it leads you. Come back to what you have written later on and ask yourself what it tells you about your own attitude to exploring the unknown. You may be able to identify fear and/ or anger in the story.

This sort of exercise is easy to turn into joke. If that was your choice, perhaps this is in itself an interesting example of resistance!

CHAPTER SIX

Singing and sailing

At this stage in the journey, when the beginning lies behind and the end is a long way ahead, a sort of sea shanty can be heard. It is made up of certain questions, repeated and restated in different ways, handed from member to member around the group. Sometimes it is sung in unison, sometimes in a more elaborate harmony with solo parts. Every group adapts the traditional version to its own unique voice, but the chorus is fairly consistent. It goes;

"What's the group for? Why are we doing this? What are we supposed to do?"

It is always interesting to reflect upon the circumstances in which the group start singing this. It can be used in a variety of ways—for example, to clarify, to redirect, to obstruct, and to provide comfort in stormy weather. Assuming, however, that this is one of the first times that the chorus has been around in the group, I want to respond to it directly. There are some answers available to the questions, which might help the group members in their task of rowing and/or sailing their boat.

FAQS

Q. What are we supposed to do?
1.   Relate to each other. This means talking and listening openly, reacting congruently, and connecting.

2. Reflect upon all this relating. This means discussing it in the group, taking it home and writing about it in a personal journal, thinking about it, sharing appropriate aspects with others.

3. Reflecting upon the whole process within the group. This means noticing the links, the patterns, the sore spots, the emotional colour and the behaviour of the group-as-a-whole.

Q. Why are we doing this?

1. To learn about your own characteristic patterns of relating. This includes, recognising when you are behaving in ingrained familiar ways, seeing the consequences of your behaviour, and understanding something of their origin.

2. To experiment with alternative styles of relating within the group, in order to increase your range of responses and develop flexibility.

3. To learn about other people's characteristic patterns of relating, to recognise the consequences of their behaviour, and to understand something of their origin.

4. To develop an attitude of openness towards yourself and others and an interest in the complexities of human relationships.

5. To become competent, self-reflexive therapists able to relate at depth to clients.

Q. What is the group for?

1. The group provides the context within which all of the above take place. Learning about oneself cannot take place in isolation. We are who we are in the context of others.

2. To demonstrate our fundamental interconnectedness.

3. Every group is constructed by its members. This provides a unique challenge for every student to take responsibility for the shape and the journey that the group goes on.

4. To provide the opportunity to struggle with the task of personal growth and development, as our clients must do.

These questions and answers underline the relationship between individual growth and group development. We learn about others and ourselves through relating and reflecting upon the process of relating. The type of shared interpersonal space that any context provides will always affect these learning possibilities. For example, the learning zone provided by a group will be different from that provided in a one-to-one relationship.

In a one-to-one relationship, the context may facilitate a detailed exploration of one particular history, the development of an intense emotional relationship, and the gratifications of being the focus of attention. In a group, we learn how we operate with others and how our own history, whatever it may be, is played out in relationships. There is less time for every member to explore their own story in detail, and more opportunity to experience and observe the outcomes of the story.

Both are routes that provide ways of understanding the self and others, and although different, will intersect at many points. The claim that "I can only develop in a one-to-one relationship" is rarely accurate in any objective sense. The group context can offer genuine opportunities for growth and development for most people. The exceptions are those people who are at a very early stage developmentally and need the emotional equivalent of breast feeding—an intense one-to-one experience without competition from siblings. Hopefully the selection process on any counselling and psychotherapy course will protect this vulnerable person from joining the course.

Assuming then, that all the members are psychologically robust enough to use the group, the task ahead lies in learning more about the group context and what it can offer. So far the work here has concentrate upon relating and reflecting as individual members of the group—learning to row. Now comes the time to think about group process and the possibility of sailing.

The group-as-a-whole

Things happen in groups just because of the group setting. Sea shanties, for example, come out of a group experience. The first chapter explored the relationship between the person and the group and introduced the idea of the individual being a "fragment of a group". In any group that meets regularly, as the PD group does, these fragments join together to form another unique group. Here, the new group will be shaped and coloured by the patterns of the significant groups in the life history of the members.

In a family group, much of the communication is unspoken. We learn the silent language of the family, both receiving and transmitting messages in subtle ways that do not rely upon words. For example, silences, gestures, and facial expressions can all be used with the finest of nuances to convey many emotions. As babies, we relate powerfully without words, and we never lose the ability to communicate in this way despite the acquisition of language.

When a number of students meet together to form a PD group, much of the communication therefore is happening below the surface of the words. Body language, movements, gestures, expressions, and atmospheres, send unspoken messages that can at times be very noisy.

We bring another type of communication without words into the group, which also comes from early experience. As babies, we are merged with our human emotional environment without the boundaries of self and other. Emotions here are collective experiences, rather than "mine" or "yours". The ability to discriminate "my feeling" from "your feeling" is a complex learnt process that comes with age and development. This overlays our earlier experience but does not eliminate it. We retain the capacity to inhabit a shared emotional space.

Under the surface of the PD group lies the shared, collective emotional environment. Emotions can be experienced mutually and collectively without clearly "belonging" to a particular person. This can at times be confusing and disorienting, but gradually the group members will be able to recognise the experience and put it to use in the group.

Zoë noticed that Geoff seemed quite agitated. He kept moving in his chair and playing with the bottle of water he had brought into the group. It was difficult to catch his eye—he seemed determined to look at the floor all the time. As Zoë looked round the circle she caught sight of Hayden also looking at Geoff. They were now the only two men in the group, as Danny had left the course last week.

Deb was talking about her father who had cancer. She was speaking quickly but quietly, and Zoë struggled to hear what she was saying. She was struck by the way in which Deb punctuated her speech with sudden high-pitched laughs. It didn't seem at all funny to Zoë.

Jill was asking Deb to repeat something. She leant forward so that she could hear better, and in doing so, blocked Zoë's view of part of the group.

Suddenly Zoë found herself filling with tears, for no reason as far as she could see. She struggled to hold them back, until Sandy suddenly blurted out—

"I feel so sad—I just want to cry. I don't know what's happening here, it feels awful!"

These sorts of experiences are not unusual in groups. They are usually explained, even in humanistic trainings, in language taken from psychodynamic theory. Concepts such as transference and counter transference, projection, identification, projective identification and introjection are called upon to explain the "movement" of emotion from one person to another. There is, however, another way of understanding what is taking place here.

Something difficult, possibly life threatening, is happening in the main story about Deb's father. There is something troubling Geoff and various members are aware of this. Another member has just left the group, and we know nothing of the circumstances. Zoë becomes cut off from part of the group and instantly fills up with tears. Sandy then puts into words what Zoë is feeling. There are strong, shared emotions of both anxiety and sadness—perhaps fear—in the group.

Group analytic theory has a concept called "contagion", which describes a situation in which members "catch" emotions from each other like a virus. That would be one way of thinking about this event in the group. I would argue, however, that all the concepts that involve transferring feeling from one individual to another miss a key factor. Sometimes emotion is not passed around like the flu, but simultaneously exists in all the group members. It is a collective, shared emotion—a pool that everyone is swimming in together.

Zoë was quite shaken by the group that evening. She wrote about it in her journal, reflecting upon how it could have happened. She found herself doodling in the margins of her notebook, and thinking about her own father, who had died 4 years previously. They hadn't got on particularly well and she had been surprised by how much his death had affected her. She wrote about this in the journal, linking it with Deb's father. She still wasn't clear whether or not Deb's father was actually dying, but Deb was obviously worried. Then she put down her pen and let her thoughts play out.

What was going on for Geoff? Was that something about fathers too? Thinking about him, she realised that he and Danny would always go around together. He seemed lost somehow on his own. So maybe it was about Danny leaving. Zoë had liked Danny, but it hadn't occurred to her until she was writing that she might be missing him too. It was the right thing to leave, she thought. He would have made a terrible counsellor—always giving advice and reassuring people. But he was warm and generous—not like her father. Maybe he had been a sort of father figure in the group. Then why didn't anyone in the group talk about Danny's absence, Zoë wondered?

I'm starting to see some connections here, she thought, about fathers, and about losing them. Next week I'm going to tell the group what I've made of it all and see if it connects with anyone else. It'll be interesting to find out what was going on with Sandy too—I'll ask her about it.

Here Zoë has been able to use the experience to reflect upon possible connections both for herself and for the group. She has asked herself some key questions to arrive at this point, which can in their own way be seen as another type of sea shanty. This time the refrain goes something like—

"What is happening to me right now? How do I feel? What thoughts are going through my head?"

The following lines are then about the group.

"What is happening in the group right now? How does it feel? What is being communicated?"

The ability to ask both sets of questions and to be open to the possible answers is of enormous importance. Once a significant proportion of the group members have reached this stage, then the group can work much more effectively.

The places that the group can reach are at the same time places that its members can access. Learning about the group, in other words, is also learning about oneself. Being able to work on both of these dimensions gives the group a much more powerful thrust. It is as if, after some time rowing, the crew discover that the boat has a sail. Once the sail is unfurled, then the possibilities of speed and distance are greatly magnified.

Sailing along

Sailing and rowing strongly have much in common. The group in both of these modes is travelling into deeper waters and exploring challenging territories. It might take a while before the group members recognise the sensation, but once identified it can provide valuable information about what is happening in the group. A group that is working has a different atmosphere from one that is avoiding work, for whatever interesting reason.

Imagine a group in which all the members seem actively engaged in a discussion. There are different viewpoints, but everyone is contributing to a conversation that has emotional energy. Members are involved not because they feel they ought to contribute but because the subject has in some way caught hold of them. The conversation passes from member to member around the group, and the presence of facilitator seems almost an irrelevance. The group are too busy talking to each other to bother about the facilitator at this point. It may be impossible to say what the group are doing, but there is a strong sense that they are doing something valuable.

Now imagine the group at a different point. Three members are having a thoughtful conversation about an incident that one of them has described, involving conflict with her teenage daughter. Two other members appear interested and engaged, although they are not contributing much. One member is very obviously gazing out of the window, and another is studying his fingernails. It seems clear that whilst some members are rowing hard, others are not. The sails have not been unfurled at this point.

There will be a different atmosphere in the group room from the one described earlier. These atmospheres, or emotional colours and tones, are important types of communication, and need to be taken seriously if the boat is going to travel any distance.

"What is happening to me right now? How do I feel? What thoughts are going through my head?"

"What is happening in the group right now? How does it feel? What is being communicated?"

If someone in the group is able to ask these questions and put their own responses into the group, then it becomes possible to broaden and deepen the conversation. As a consequence, it could emerge that the person looking out of the window is angry because no-one has asked her about an important event that she mentioned in the previous session. She is feeling let down and left out. This opens up a whole possible group conversation about being heard, being taken seriously, wanting to be the centre of attention, and so forth.

The man cleaning his fingernails might take the group in another direction. He says he is bored. He is challenged by another member who recollects an earlier disclosure about this man's own teenage daughter. He then talks more about why he did not want to be a part of the group discussion and the emotions that he feared it might provoke. The conversation in the group then widens to father-daughter interactions and conflicts in adolescence. Sulking is mentioned as an important aspect of adolescent communication, and the woman who had been staring out of the window recognised that at that moment, she had been behaving like the adolescent in the group.

Now this has become a group that is working hard, and the atmosphere will have changed. In a way, the whole group has been engaged in the shared topic of adolescence and parenting from the beginning. Those members who seemed disconnected had important experiences that were very relevant to the work that the rest of the group were doing. Whilst these experiences were unspoken and not integrated into the conversation, the group was held back in its attempts to travel. Once the unspoken material was articulated and put into the group, the sails unfurled and the group set off through the water!

The new chorus

This chapter began with a repetitive chorus of "what are we supposed to be doing here?" Having taken the question at face value, and answered it as clearly as possible, the group and its members need to move on. If the question is a genuine search for information, then it needs to translate itself into a different form that is capable of producing insight and movement.

"What is happening to me right now? How do I feel? What thoughts are going through my head?"

"What is happening in the group right now? How does it feel? What is being communicated?"

These are the key questions that can open the way for exploration and travel. Like a chorus in a sea shanty, the words are simple and easily remembered. Like a sea shanty, everyone can take part, whatever their voice, and the effect becomes more powerful as more people join in. Asking the questions and thinking about the answers is a shared task. Although it may be valuable to reflect individually and silently at times, generally it is more productive to put the answers or confusions into the group through language.

Each member has a limited number of perceptions, reactions and ideas, which need the responses of others to become coherent pictures and new discoveries. In the PD group, no single person has the complete answer to any question. The members who voice their own here- and- now experiences of the group not only move the boat in the water, but discover that in all likelihood they are not alone. The experience of members is linked, and a strong feeling in any particular member will have meaning and relevance for the others.

Shifting focus—the look out and the cabin crew

It is this constantly shifting focus from group to individual and back, that is most likely to unfurl the sails. Being able to reflect upon what is happening as a group, as well as what is happening as a member, will provide the energy and understanding to drive the boat for-wards. A group member acts at times like a look-out, scanning the sea for clues about direction, weather conditions, underwater dangers and so on. They have the telescope to see into the distance and get a sense of perspective on the course that the boat is set upon. Then at other times, they are cabin crew, completely focused upon what is happening in the boat.

As a counsellor or psychotherapist it is vitally important to be able to hold in mind both the particular and the contextual. Learn-ing to look around and within, and to switch fluently between these perspectives, is another skill that can be learnt in the PD group. In the group there are continuous examples of the interconnection between the individual member and the group-as-a-whole. In the example used earlier, the group loses a particular member, which has an effect on both the group itself and upon individual members. The two aspects always work together. Being able to use both perspectives is like looking down the telescope from both ends. It is possible to see both the intimate detail and also the distant horizon, and to switch readily between the two.

The end of term is three weeks away. The group has been struggling to get going this session. Jo feels very tired and just wants to go home. Sara is absent, after having been the centre of a conversation in the previous group about feeling picked on. Dee is staring at everyone's shoes in the circle. Jena has her arms folded, head down and staring at the floor. Barti is looking at the facilitator hopefully. Mark and Doug are talking about the latest assignment, with Mark giving Doug some tips about useful websites to check out.

The facilitator asks the group what is going on. There is a silence.

Jo. *I'm just really tired, that's all. To be honest, I'm waiting for seven o'clock so we can all go home.*

Mark. *Well I thought I was having a useful conversation with Doug, which you (looking at the facilitator) have just interrupted!*

Barti. *I thought you had finished. I didn't think John interrupted at all. What did you think, Doug?*

Doug. *Um, well, um, I don't know really. Mark obviously had more to say or he wouldn't have felt interrupted. Yeah, it was helpful stuff—thanks Mark.*

Jena. *I'm with Jo here. Roll on seven o'clock.*

Barti. *Why do you say that Jena? You look really fed up.*

Jena. *Don't know—I just feel this is all a waste of time today. It's probably nothing really. Maybe because that talk we've just had was so boring. It was hard to stay awake.*

Jo. *Yes, it was the worst one we've had so far. Normally they get us to do some exercises or something, but she just went on and on and on. Solid information—I switched off well before half way.*

Mark. *I thought it was good, actually. I learnt a lot of useful things about telephone counselling and she gave us a very comprehensive handout and bibliography. I thought it much better than the previous one on nature and ecology—I found that very tedious.*

Dee. *That was the best one, Mark! How can you say it was tedious?*

Mark. *Because that is exactly how I experienced it, Dee.*

"What is happening in the group right now? How does it feel? What is being communicated?"

This exercise asks you to apply this set of questions to the group described above, but in a more detailed manner.

1.   How do you imagine it felt in the group-as-a-whole?
2.   Look at the context of this group session and identify any interesting landmarks, rocks in the water, weather conditions, etc.

3. What connections can be made between the answers to
    the first two questions?
4. Do you think that the feeling tone changes during this
    episode? If so, at what point or points do you think it
    shifts?
5. Can you identify a theme or themes?
6. Imagine that the group can speak as if it is one person—
    that it has one voice. What might it be saying here?

Only read the following section when you have tried to answer
the questions for yourself. Your ideas are much more valuable than
anyone else's at this point, and there are no "correct" answers but
rather multiple possibilities. What follows is a very partial response
to the questions to give an example of the sort of thinking that you
might apply. There is much more that might be said.

How do you imagine it felt in the group-as-a-whole?
- Heavy, uncomfortable, lifeless.

Look at the context of this group session and identify any interesting
landmarks, rocks in the water, weather conditions, etc.
- Things brought into group from previous teaching session.
- Only three meetings before a break.
- Something not dealt with from the previous week.
- A significant absent member.

What connections can be made between the answers to the first two
questions?
- Bringing the group to life by addressing the important issues
  might be dangerous.

Does the feeling tone change?
- There are flickers of irritation between Mark and Dee, plus
  Mark's comment about John.

Can you identify a theme or themes?
- Being picked on.
- Difference.

Imagine that the group can speak as if it is one person—that it has one voice. What might it be saying here?

There's something angry and uncomfortable here that I want to cut off from.

It is not important that your answers match these. The point is to begin to ask these sorts of questions about the group and its members. For many students it will represent a different style of thinking, and like any new pattern requires practice and reinforcement to become established.

Think about your previous PD group meeting and practise looking at it from both ends of the telescope. Ask those key questions both of yourself and of the group-as-a-whole. Recording your responses in your learning journal may help you to keep them in mind when the group meets again.

This next meeting will be the opportunity to practice in real time what has been learnt—an opportunity to develop the ability to shift focus between group and individual, and to ask the key questions.

CHAPTER SEVEN

Conflict

"*C*onflict" is a word that is always in the news. It stretches across a wide territory that includes the bloody and butcherous civil war as well as the quietly persistent personal dilemma. It can encompass both unmitigated destruction and creative tension.

What does the word mean for us? What images are brought to mind when we hear it?

Every member of every PD group will have experienced some form of conflict. This unique personal history, in conjunction with that of the wider family and cultural group, will shape the meaning of conflict for each group member. It will also be coloured by the ever present media representations of conflict around the world that are impossible to avoid in our contemporary society.

Conflict in the PD group is inevitable and potentially very healthy, but like everything else in the group can become entangled and unproductive. It certainly helps to keep hold of a sense of proportion. Sensibilities and egos will be wounded, and distressing confrontations may occur both with others and the self. It is not an environment free from emotional pain, but a PD group is not a civil war zone and the casualties are not fatal.

A sense of humour helps too, and can provide a valuable counter balance to any tendency to dramatise. Being able to laugh, particularly at oneself, can restore a sense of proportion, release tension and change an atmosphere. Of course, humour can have negative

75

aspects, but it also has a valuable role as a pin to stick into the balloon of drama that can sometimes inflate around conflict in PD groups. "Learning to row" can refer to the task of moving the boat along with oars, but if pronounced differently, means learning to handle conflict. The two areas of learning are mutually supportive and interdependent. It is not possible to row the boat very far without encountering a row or argument. Neither is it possible to understand, defuse, or deconstruct a conflict or row without having some skills as a rower in the group boat.

What is acceptable?

Some people are comfortable with conflict and have developed skills in this form of communication. Anyone watching the televised proceedings of the House of Commons will see two groups seated opposite each other engaging in ritualised confrontations where the ability to verbally attack one's opponent is deemed a positive asset. Popular team sports such as football and rugby are other ritualised expressions of conflict. Conflict in all these places is circumscribed by rules that lay down what is acceptable and unacceptable, with clear penalties and consequences for transgressions of the boundaries.

The PD group is similar in that it needs clear boundaries to enable conflict to take place without escalating into chaos and violence. Sometimes this is discussed in the early boundary-setting phase of the group, and sometimes it swims into view only when conflict actually becomes expressed.

It needs to be unequivocally clear that physical conflict is completely unacceptable. Both group and facilitator need to be absolutely confident that this is a boundary that must not be crossed and that any transgression will not be tolerated. In a PD group this is not a likely occurrence, but that does not mean that members do not at times feel physically threatened and need the security of this solid boundary. Any sort of physical violence, such as slamming doors or kicking chairs is likely to create powerful emotional responses in the group, and the members need to be quite confident that this sort of acting out will not escalate into physical conflict.

But apart form this one very clear boundary, does the group need further protection from conflict? The more fearful the group members, the more restrictions they will want to place around conflict and how it is to be expressed. The more restrictions there are, the greater likelihood of conflict going under the surface and being expressed indirectly or passively. If, for example, the group insist that members talk rather than shout, and treat each other respectfully at all times, they are in effect saying "don't bring any real conflict into here—we can't cope with it". When people are genuinely angry with each other, they are not always respectful and quiet. Neither are clients, and there needs to be some level of tolerance for unguarded emotional expression if relationships are to develop beyond superficial politeness.

The difficult area comes in assessing when verbal conflict turns into verbal abuse. Conflict over a particular issue can escalate into generalised conflict where the distinction is lost between how someone behaves and how they are as a person. A group that wants to tolerate conflict in order to learn from it might unwittingly give free rein to abusive behaviour on the part of a member or members. If the group has had some discussion around this and is aware of the danger, the likelihood of it happening and/or the destructive potential can be diminished. In the last resort, this is one of the occasions where the facilitator has a responsibility to the group and its members to intervene decisively whenever she or he feels the conflict is turning into an opportunity for abusive behaviour.

This is an opportunity to reflect upon your own attitudes and experiences. The questions are prompts to help you begin think about this aspect of yourself, and will hopefully lead you into asking further questions of your own.

What did you learn about conflict in the family as a child? Was it openly or passively expressed, and were there particular people who expressed it?

Was it acceptable for you to express anger? What are your memories of "winning" and "losing"?

What were the acceptable styles of conflict for family members? Were there differences around gender, age, ability, status or other variables?

Was conflict seen as positive, negative, or neutral? What was its characteristic outcome?

Can you identify this childhood learning in your style of dealing with conflict as an adult?

If the answer is "no", what was the source of the new learning, and what did it teach you about conflict?

What do you think has had the most influence upon your attitudes to conflict?

What do you see as your strengths and weaknesses in conflict situations?

What are the changes you would like to make in the course of the PD group?

Where is the conflict?

This is a far more complicated question than it seems at first sight. Conflict can take place between group members, between sub groups of members, between a member and the facilitator, between all the members or some of the members and the facilitator, between the group-as-a-whole and the course or institution, between the facilitator and the course or institution, between the group and the members, and between the social and cultural groups that come together within the PD group setting. The conflict can be between people or within people or both, located in the past as well as the present, and projected into the future. There is a huge tangle of possibilities here, and the only way to make any sense of it is to pull out one thread and see where it takes us. Learning to manage one of the threads can not only provide a model for the others but also demonstrate the constant ambiguity in locating exactly where the conflict belongs. An obvious place to begin is to look at conflict between group members.

Conflict between group members

There is always conflict between members, even in the most seemingly friendly and co-operative group. The group that never argues does not demonstrate an absence of conflict but rather an intense fear of it. Any relationship that develops beyond the superficial will come up against some point of tension. People we care about bother us, and we bother them. The key issue is how that is expressed and what can be learnt from it to enable relationships to grow and develop.

Our early experiences may have taught us to sidestep and swallow conflict, or to stand and fight, or any of the multiple alternatives between the extremes. The task in the PD group is to get beyond these programmed responses into new territory and new possibilities.

Breda was looking tense, sitting with her arms folded and legs crossed. The group were discussing the latest assignment and gradually the conversation petered out. The silence was eventually broken by the facilitator commenting on how uncomfortable Breda seemed to be. She replied in an unconvincing way that she was fine.

Sue began to talk about an incident in her week when she had felt very angry and upset with her manager at work. Various other members were asking her about the incident, when Mandy said she was feeling really uncomfortable about Breda, who had remained silent and uncommunicative.

In response to further inquiries, Breda said in a clipped and spiky manner—

"I decided that I wouldn't say anything this week. I don't see the point. Whenever I do say anything I feel as if it is a complete waste of time, and then I get upset. There's no point in that, I decided."

Jane asked if it had anything to do with the previous week when they were talking about mothers. She had noticed that Breda seemed to close down right at the end of the group.

"I wasn't going to say anything, but yes, I did go away feeling very upset".

"Upset? Maybe angry?" asked the facilitator.

Breda pulled a face.

"I suppose I was a bit angry—maybe I still am. I felt as if I'd told the group something really important about my relationship with my mother and it was completely ignored. Sue started to talk about her mother and that was the end of it. So I just shut up!"

Karen said "I feel terrible, I can't even remember what you said, Breda. It just didn't register as something so important. I'm sorry I didn't mean to ignore you, I just never realised."

Breda looked tearful and Mandy passed her a tissue.

"I feel that I must be such a dull person, and no-one wants to listen to me. You'd all rather hear about Sue."

Sue said stoutly, "Oh that's just nonsense. Everyone gets the same opportunity here. Nobody gets listened to any more than anyone else—at least if you speak up, that is."

Breda's tears turned to sobs. In a slightly hysterical voice, she spluttered—
"There you are, you've just done it again—you never take any notice of
my feelings -you just crash in and all the attention turns to you and
whatever I was trying to say gets pushed to one side. You've done that to
me so many times in this group and I'm sick of it!"

It has taken some teasing out, but at last the conflict between Breda
and Sue is in the open. Now the group has an opportunity to
acknowledge it, comment upon it and try to make sense of what is
happening.

When you read this example, what was your response?
Did you feel sympathy for any of the characters?
Did you feel annoyed with any of them?
Imagine you are a member of the group who has not yet
spoken. What impact does the conflict have upon you?
What would your contribution be at this point?
What would be your preferred outcome?

The group in the example may seem very lost at this point. Some
members will want to get away from any emotional discomfort as
quickly as possible, and may try to console and reassure Breda.
Others may find themselves on one side or the other in the conflict,
and contribute further to the argument. Some may withdraw into
silence, whilst others may be provoked into expressing their own
anger. As a member sitting in the group it can be confusing, worrying, frustrating, exciting—and this will relate to earlier experiences
of conflict and resolution in other groups, particularly the family.
What follows is not a set of rules but a loose framework that might
be helpful as a guide in these circumstances.

If the group is to take this conflict seriously, it will need to gather
evidence. Sue is being accused of taking the focus away from Breda
onto herself, on a number of unspecified occasions including the one
just experienced in the group. Both Breda and Sue need the
opportunity to describe their own experiences of these incidents.
They may not at this stage be able to hear each other, but the group

can hear them, and ensure that both sides of the argument are given time in the group.

When Sue and Breda have given their versions, it is important that the other group members add their perceptions of the events under discussion. They are the witnesses to the conflict and have an important role in building up the overall picture. This is serious rowing for every member and challenges those whose characteristic pattern is to "not get involved". In this way, the group can build a multi dimensional picture of the relationship between Breda and Sue, set in the context of the group network.

During this process of collecting up the jigsaw pieces, the emotional tone of the group may cool down. If this does not happen, the group may find it difficult to keep working at the picture whilst strong feelings are washing through the boat. At some point, the group needs to begin thinking about what is happening rather than being overwhelmed by emotion. If too many oars are splashing water into the boat, then what is needed is a pause, when everyone rests on their oars and allows the boat to just bob in the water. Sometimes the facilitator needs to intervene, acknowledging the strong feelings but encouraging the group to sit back and breathe for a moment. Pressing the pause button to freeze the frame is another useful metaphor. Not all the members may stop splashing, but if there are enough who can begin to think, then the boat can stabilise.

From the conversation in the group certain "pieces of evidence" emerge. Nobody had recognised that Breda was sharing something of such importance when she spoke in the previous session. As Mandy said, "It sounded very wrapped up—as if you had got it all sorted out and were just letting us know about it."

Everyone agreed that Sue spoke a lot in the group, but only Karen thought that she sometimes took over group conversations. Most members thought that Sue did a lot of work in the group, and one member admitted to feeling a bit envious of how comfortable she seemed to be in the group.

There was a recognition that the relationship between Sue and Breda had changed from being apparently warm and friendly at the start of the course to a more distant one. Sue's version was that she liked Breda but wanted to get to know others as well. Once Sue had got to know more people, Breda drifted away. Sue was not looking for a special one-to-one relationship, but she thought that Breda was, and it had felt a bit suffocating at times. She did not think she was pushing Breda out of the group conversation.

Breda was finding it difficult to get beyond being upset, but with the help of the facilitator talked more about the feelings of being excluded, ignored, and pushed away. Then Chris, a group member who had been silent up until this point, contributed a powerful personal experience of being the only child in the family who was sent away to boarding school.

Listening to Chris gave Breda the space to start to reflect. She too had powerful family experiences of being the child who was treated differently and who felt unheard. At this point, the group began to explore together the connections between the experiences brought into the group from the past, and the present situation. This linking of past and present is a key stage in understanding the events in the group, and explaining the emotional intensity of some encounters.

The group were working hard in a shared conversation about being excluded in the family, and most members were engaged and active. The facilitator had to interrupt the conversation to announce the end of the group, saying that there was much more to be said and hoped that the group would continue in the following session. The conflict was not resolved, but it had changed shape.

In the following session, Karen asked Breda how she was, and had she thought about the group during the week.

Breda replied that she had been doing a lot of reflecting and could see that there was a connection between how she felt in the group and how she felt in her family. But she was still felt angry and upset with Sue, and still felt as if Sue took over and didn't listen to her. She didn't really want to talk about it any more, as she had taken up a lot of the group's time already.

Sue then said that she too had been thinking a lot about it, and she did want to talk more about it.

Conflicts can take time to understand and resolve, and are rarely genuinely cleared away in one group session. The group may manage to do some work on the issue but then come up against another obstacle. It can be like untying a very complex knot, requiring persistence and patience. One of the few certainties in the life of the PD group is that conflict does not go away because it is not spoken about. It may be stowed away in the boat out of sight, but will spill out again at some point in the journey.

Difference and similarity

Popular wisdom has it that we get on well with people who are similar to us, and are likely to fall out with those who are different. During the course of a PD group, this idea will be seriously challenged and probably overturned. It is often the people who are like us in some way that cause the most difficulty. Of course, we do not recognise the similarity, and may not want to recognise it. Here lies the source of many conflicts, which the challenge of personal growth and development can uncover.

Sometimes it is clear to most of the group that a conflict rests upon similarity. When the group member who tells long and rambling stories gets exasperated by another member "not getting to the point", or when the member with the sharp tongue is angered by an acid response, then others can see the likenesses. It is as if one member holds up a mirror to another, reflecting some aspect that otherwise cannot be seen. Clear and repeated feedback from the group can enable the participants to recognise this similarity and integrate it into their image of themselves, rather than only see it in others.

There are less obvious examples of this process of mirroring, which require more work to uncover.

Sue has a responsible administrative job at the local university. She has a partner but they do not live together, and she shares her house with two post-graduate students now that her children have left home. She has a wide circle of friends and is an active member of the local environmental pressure group.

Breda lives with her husband and daughter, and works part time as a bookkeeper in her husband's business. Her younger sister lives nearby and Breda spends much of her time trying to support her through various domestic, financial and emotional crises. Breda's main interest has always been her home and family, and she has only recently begun to develop her own interests in painting and drawing.

Here are two women with different strengths and different life styles. Sue appears more independent and socially confident. Breda comes across as lacking confidence in herself, but good at looking after others. So perhaps an element in their conflict comes from this disparity, with the less confident person looking for someone stronger to attach herself to, and the more confident person experiencing that as constraining. Or perhaps it is just a clash between the inward looking home loving introvert, and the outgoing sociable extrovert. It might be tempting for the PD group, having made these links, to feel that the conflict was now understood. Most members will know, however, that relationships are rarely that simple.

Sue's parents separated when she was 9 years old. Her two older sisters stayed with her mother, and she and her younger brother lived with their father. When she was 14, and her older sisters had left home, she went back to live with her mother and stepfather. Her mother soon became very demanding, expecting Sue to care for the younger stepchildren, and Sue was very unhappy. As soon as she was 16, she moved into a flat with her boyfriend. They married young and separated when their own three children were all under five years old. The eldest, the only boy, stayed with his father, and the girls stayed with Sue. All now live away from home.

Breda is the eldest of four daughters, whose mother died when she was 13. She took on the role of mothering the family until father remarried when she was 15. Her sisters seemed to get on well with their stepmother but Breda resented her. When she was 16 the family moved to Ireland, leaving Breda with a friend in order to stay on at school and take "A" levels. The family did not settle in Ireland, returning two years later, but by this time Breda had a place at college and never moved back in with them. She met her first boyfriend, later to become her husband, on the first day of college. They have one daughter who plans to go travelling in the autumn.

When we look for similarity rather than difference, some powerful shared experiences emerge. Both were young girls who were separated from their mothers at puberty. This major loss was then compounded by an experience of rejection. Sue was sent away from her mother to live with her father, and Breda was displaced as the family's new mother by a stepmother. Subsequently another major rejection reinforced the message of the first. Sue's attempt to get close to her mother at 14 was a failure, and Breda was left behind when the rest of the family went to Ireland. They both chose a partner at a very young age, searching for security in a new family base of their own.

For both of them too, there were siblings who were treated very differently. Sue's sisters stayed with her mother, and Breda's sisters went to Ireland as part of a family unit. They may share an inter-nalised message that goes something like "mothers let you down, and sisters get more love than you do". Although they have taken different paths to come to terms with this message, it is a fundamental shared experience. When they encounter each other in an emotionally intense environment such as counselling or psychotherapy training, these similarities are recognised. At first, the recognition is out of their awareness, unconsciously affecting their behaviour towards each other. Their original family groups are similar enough to emotionally experience themselves as fragments of the same group.

In this way Breda can play the part of the mother who at first seems to care but then becomes needy and demanding—Sue's mother. Sue can play the part of the mother who offers closeness and then is not available—Breda's mother. Breda can be for Sue the older sister who mother loved more. For Breda, Sue can play the part of a younger sister who did not lose the family. Conflict between these two women cannot be understood without reference back to these crucial early experiences.

If the group is working well, in the process of exploring and digesting this material someone will voice the realization that these two group members have very similar fears about rejection and about competition. Although they have managed these fears in different ways, fundamentally they are alike in these respects. This point of recognition repeats itself in group life again and again. The root of conflict is often a shared fear or anxiety, which is concealed beneath differing styles of self-protection. The similarity is only revealed after serious exploration and much hard work in the group.

This is an exercise that focuses upon the self and the internal landscape. As always in groups, it is then important to redirect the focus onto the others and the external landscape. What is happening in the group?

The group context

Although conflict may appear to be a two person dynamic, this is never the case. It is impossible to divorce the conflict from the context of the group. The web of interconnections means that strands of conflict, experiences of rejection, envy and competitiveness pervade the entire group. All members are implicated, and all have important things to learn from the conflict.

The issues or themes that are expressed through conflict are relevant for the group as a whole. The envy and competitiveness revealed in the Sue–Breda conflict, for example, reflects an important issue in the group. It may lie out of awareness until the conflict erupts, but then can be talked about and worked with. A conflict can be an expression of a group concern as much as an individual challenge. If group members can reflect upon their own attitudes and experiences around the issues in any conflict, then the ownership of the "problem" can pass from the antagonistic couple to the whole group. In this way, conflict between members can be a positive venting of underlying frustrations or difficulties that have not until this point been aired in the group. Groups that leave the problem with the couple are backing away from important personal issues and missing opportunities to learn about themselves.

Again what is important is the need to continually change focus— from the individual to the group, from the group to the individual. Events in the group cannot be understood without paying attention to the context of the group, and also the wider context within which the group operates.

Imagine you are sitting in your own PD group. Look around the circle and identify the person or persons who you least like or who irritate you.

What is it that you dislike?

Think first about their physical appearance and body language. Then focus upon their style of clothing, and the image that they portray. Next concentrate on their voice—its tone, accent, and pitch.

Having completed a detailed physical survey and noted the aspects which you dislike or which irritate you, move on to think about attitudes and perceptions.

What does this person say that annoys you? Are there characteristic phrases that grate or is it more about an attitude? Do they express ideas that you disagree with? Is it the way in which they relate to others that irritates you?

These questions are attempting to identify the factors that produce a feeling of dislike or irritation. It may be difficult to find a clear answer, but important to keep investigating. This is the stage of gathering evidence and clarifying details, which is necessary to enable you to move on to the fascinating questions about past and present.

The usual question is "Who does this person remind you of?" That may indeed be a very helpful question, but often it draws a blank. Obvious similarities are easily recognised, and these are easier to work with and understand. Often however, similarities are not global but particular. One specific aspect, such as the tone of voice, may be the key link with some aspect of a previous encounter. All the evidence that you have gathered needs to be looked at in this way. We are often reminded of something or someone not by a complete picture but by some small detail.

What do you know about this person's life? Do you have some similar experiences?

In what ways is the person who you do not like, similar to you? Our dislikes and irritations can tell us much about ourselves if we are open to this possibility.

The last question is the most difficult and asking someone else's opinion might be helpful.

CHAPTER EIGHT

Underlying division and difference

Any attempt to understand what happens in a PD group has to constantly wrestle with the interplay of the big picture with the little picture. The group is part of a course, which is part of a college, which is part of an educational system, which is part of a society, which is part of a culture, which is part of a country, and so on. It is one small circle positioned in a sea of other overlapping and concentric circles, and it can never be understood without reference to this overall view.

The seabed

If the PD group is like a boat, this is the point in the journey at which there is the possibility of hitting the rocks or becoming trapped. The seabed is full of dangerous fissures and jagged outcrops, creating powerfully turbulent waters. Any boat venturing in these waters will do well to have some sort of map.

The society in which the PD group operates is discriminatory, unjust and unequal. It is a society where some groups of people have more economic wealth, more access to resources and opportunities and more influence in determining the distribution of these resources. The key criteria that determine membership of these more powerful groups are race, gender, age, disability, ethnicity and class. Although particular individuals may transcend these barriers, the categories remain durable and potent.

Members of PD groups generally wish to create a fair and just society within their groups where everyone has an equal voice.

Unfortunately, translating this wish into reality will be a great struggle. There are some enormously powerful obstacles in the way and perhaps the best that can realistically be hoped for is that these can be recognised and worked with to some degree.

The problem is ourselves. We are not separate from the society and culture we belong to, however much we would like to be. Attitudes and beliefs are not grafted on at some stage of development, but are interwoven into the structure of our personality.

Unaware, we are shaped by beliefs that are so pervasive they appear to be unquestionably right or natural. Beliefs about the respective natures of men and women, for example, are not consciously taught to us, but are absorbed from our earliest experiences. Despite years of research that challenges ideas that men and women have essential characteristic differences, the belief that "boys will be boys"—aggressive, loud, boisterous, competitive—remains ingrained in this society. It is just one example of those attitudes that derive their power from appearing to be "natural" and "normal", thus making them enormously influential.

The implication of the definition "natural" or "normal" is that it is persists through time. In fact, our ideas about what constitutes normality have altered through history. Homosexuality, for example, is still in the process of redefining itself as "normal" after decades of being described as "unnatural". In the twentieth century, firmly held convictions about women, such as their innate inability to drive, were overturned by the experiences of war. History reveals a series of shifting concepts rather then any consistent and enduring definition of what is normal or natural. We can look back in time and be shocked by the narrow mindedness or bigotry of our ancestors. Their "normality" we may now see as prejudice or ignorance, and we congratulate ourselves on our superior understanding. Sadly, we cannot see how the process applies to ourselves any more than the Victorians could in their day.

Language

We do, however, have one major clue, and that is language. Our underlying beliefs and attitudes, the woven threads of ourselves, are powerfully shaped by language. In any culture, language directs attention to certain parts of the social, emotional and political environment and ignores others .We do not use language to express a pre-existing thought, but rather the thought only becomes possible because of the available language. Different languages identify different experiences, emotions, explanatory frameworks, codes of conduct, and so forth.

Counsellors and psychotherapist have always understood the significance of words—after all, they are "talking therapies". What exactly is spoken, in what manner and context, and the meanings and associations that can be attached to these words, are the bedrock of the counselling relationship. So it is reasonable to expect both that trainees will be sensitive to language and that training will help them further appreciate its profound importance.

Using language thoughtfully leads inevitably into the realm of "political correctness". Political correctness at its best sensitises us to the needs and perceptions of others who we might "unthinkingly" offend by our use of language. It signals where the ingrained attitudes lie in wait for us, in the way that marker buoys alert the shipping to dangerous underwater reefs. We need to censor our language because it reveals how we have been structured by all our experience, both conscious and unconscious. Language reveals the fabric of ourselves that is woven through growing and living in a particular society in a particular historical time. It reveals fundamental attitudes towards the "normal/abnormal", acceptable/ unacceptable, threatening/non threatening, similar/different, powerful/weak.

Political correctness demands that we change our language. We have to be vigilant that our language does not discriminate, demean, stereotype, and offend—because that is exactly what our language does do. It expresses what we have absorbed about who we need to protect ourselves from, who threatens us though difference, who we should look up to and who we can look down upon.

The expectation that we should choose our words carefully is in many ways laudable. The problem is that learning a new language requires certain conditions if it is ever to be achieve fluency. It needs to be practiced regularly, with others, in a context where it is the dominant language form. We know that if we want to speak Italian fluently, we cannot merely insert the odd Italian word in our speech. We have to learn a completely different vocabulary and grammar structure. Even then, we will only speak it fluently if we are surrounded by other native speakers and can absorb the language rather than study it. Plus, somewhere in this process we have to start thinking in Italian—our internal linguistic frame has to change. In just the same way, the new language of political correctness will not move beyond the superficial unless these same conditions apply.

It is idealistic to suppose that everyone in the PD group is sufficiently fluent in the new language to be able to think in it. The language spoken inside each member's head is far more likely to be the mother tongue, the language that she or he was brought up in.

This is an extended exercise that continues throughout the entire chapter. It focuses upon a PD group with eight members. Information about the members will be revealed a step at a time, and further questions asked. To get the most from this exercise it is important to go with your first responses, before your internal censor has got to work! Then at a later point you can look at your own responses and reflect upon what they feed back to you about your own underlying attitudes.

The only information you have to begin with is the name, age and gender of these members.

Gloria, f, 34	Jan, f, 45
Margaret, f, 63	Paul, m, 43
Joanne, f, 30	Irma, f, 22
Vinnie, m, 29	Sheena, f, 36

a. Can you imagine any possible consequences of this patterning of age and gender in the group? Where might any alliances or conflicts arise?

b. Choose either the right or left hand column, and picture each member in your mind. Create an image of their appearance that includes body language and speech.

c. Imagine yourself in this group. Who would you sit next to, and why?

d. Now add to the mix the facilitator—David, m, 54. Create an imaginative picture of him. How might your four chosen members respond to him? How do you feel about him?

A group that can accept that all its members will have some attitudes and ideas that are "politically incorrect" will achieve far more than the group that has to insist that none of these things are present. Issues of race, gender, age, class, ethnicity, disability, and sexuality may be disguised or denied in the group, but they will nevertheless be there.

Gender and sexuality

Gender is the fundamental division in human society, and in our contemporary culture presents us with continual questions about what it means to be a "man" or "woman." Stereotypes are the answer to the question, and although each generation revisits the question and comes up with some new answers, at a deeper level society continues to reproduce beliefs about male and female that our ancestors would recognise. An example would be the continuing gendered difference in attitudes towards competition, conflict, assertiveness, rationality, empathy, and emotional disclosure.

Being a "man" or "woman" in a heterosexual world means behaving in a certain way, and having certain expectations of each other. For example, there is a widely held belief that men are more rational and less comfortable in expressing emotion than women, and that women do the emotional work in heterosexual relationships. In this way, the stereotypes not only offer a description of each category, male and female, but of how the two inter-relate. By definition, a stereotype does not deal with individual variation and subtlety, and few, if any, of the PD group members will perform as the stereotypical man or woman. But in rebelling from the stereotype we demonstrate its powerful role. It underpins the development of out own beliefs about the nature of men and women, and will be alive somewhere, at various points in the PD group.

How would you describe the difference between "man" and "woman"?
Look again at your responses to the previous exercise. Do they tell you something about your own beliefs and attitudes towards gender?

Gender comes entwined with sexuality. The stereotypes that apply in the heterosexual frame can be overturned in the homosexual. Gay culture subverts and challenges what the heterosexual group claims to be the proper order of things. There are stereotypes here too, but of a different construction—gay men are emotionally expressive, for example, or lesbians are spiky and assertive.

In the group it becomes clear that Vinnie and Jan are gay .

a. In what ways does this alter the image that you have created for them? What changes?

b   How might it affect the relationships in the group?

Age

It is easy to say that age does not matter. Like most glib formulas, it disguises another, more conflictual reality. Status, authority, respect, economic power, physical well-being, sexual desire, desirability and performance, are all amongst the factors that present or withhold opportunities according to age. In the hypothetical group, Margaret may play a range of parts depending on a whole variety of other factors, but she will always be the eldest in the group. The reality that her life has lasted three times as long as that of the youngest member, or that she is old enough to be the mother of the rest of the group cannot be written out by these other factors. It will play a part somewhere in the life of the PD group. Positive and negative echoes of older women, mothers and grandmothers, are likely to find their way into the network of group relationships via her presence in the circle.

Similarly, the reality that Irma is the youngest member will play some part. For example, she may play the role of baby in the group, the youngest in the family, the one who needs protecting, the parent's favourite, or the adult who missed out on childhood. Each possibility comes with positive or negative colourings, and can enrich the learning in the group once it can be verbalised and worked with.

Race and ethnicity

Further information is now available about the group members.

Gloria is Afro Caribbean, who came to England when she was 2 years old.

Margaret is English, born in Singapore where her father worked.

Joanne is English, brought up in a single parent family in a deprived area.

Vinnie is British Asian. His father is a consultant oncologist.

Jan is Anglo-Irish. Her father died when she was 6, and her mother is a nurse.

Paul is English, adopted as a baby

Irma is Polish, coming to England when she was 4 years old.

Sheena is British Asian.

David, the facilitator, is Canadian.

With each new set of information—

a.   Adjust your image of your 4 chosen members and notice what exactly changes.
b.   Pay attention to the way in which your feelings towards the character alter.
c.   Reflect upon the way in which relationships that you have so far considered might alter. Where do you see possible alliances and conflicts now?

Divisions that follow racial and ethnic lines dictate the shape of the contemporary world. From the global to the local, there is nowhere unaffected by the powerful emotions that ethnic difference generates. In many parts of the world, ethnic identity is more crucial than national identity. Being Catalan may take precedence over being Spanish, being Welsh over being British, Kurdish rather than Iranian, and so on and on. The ethnic group, which gives us our identity, generates a fierce emotional allegiance whenever it is threatened, and the world is full of violent conflicts that demonstrate this.

It is not a subject that can be ignored. Issues concerning racial and ethnic difference will form a part of any counselling and psychotherapy training, and the course will hopefully attempt to increase awareness and sensitivity. It does not imply any criticism of the teaching to acknowledge that attitudes and emotions surrounding racial and ethnic difference are profoundly ingrained, and like all our basic foundational attitudes, resistant to change.

So it is reasonable to expect that ethnic difference will play a significant part in any PD group. It is an area that can generate high anxiety. Few people are comfortable with an image of themselves as racists and many like to feel that it is an issue that they have already "dealt with". The outcome in the PD group can be stifling, as a lot of significant material gets censored and the group struggles through lack of authenticity.

Intertwined with ethnicity may come religion. Add the following information to your images and reflect upon its impact in the group.

Gloria and Margaret would both describe themselves as active Christians.
Vinnie is Muslim.
Sheena is Hindu.
Irma is Catholic.
Jan comes from a Catholic family but is now a Quaker.
Paul calls himself an atheist.

Religious belief comes in many styles, from fundamentalism to liberal tolerance. Any firmly held conviction that is not open to modification presents a group with a challenge. It may be an aspect that is not available for development, so the task becomes how to deal with something fixed and immovable. It is as if the boat comes up against a large rock, or group of rocks, and has to learn how to negotiate around them without becoming shipwrecked or trapped. There is a lot of learning to be had from this manoeuvre, however frustrating it may seem at the time.

Class

If the PD group is struggling with major conflicts rooted in race, class might seem unimportant. Like age, it is one of the divisions in this society that can easily be underestimated but continues to play a key role in relationships. There is enough information already available about the group in the exercise to consider the role of social class.

Look again at the information again from the perspective of social class. What new possibilities does this introduce into your picture of the group? How might it colour the relationships between any of the members?

In my picture of Margaret, for example, I have imagined her family to be an upper class, expatriot, and privileged group. In my mind I hear Margaret talking in very proper, correct English, rather like the Queen. The scenario is then easy to construct whereby Joanne finds her incredibly irritating. Joanne, in my picture, comes from a poor working class culture and is proud of the fact that all her achievements have come through her own efforts, with no advantages of birth or upbringing.

Your picture may be very different. The point is that class remains a point of contact and conflict, and not just in the British culture. Every society makes fine discriminations between people and orders them into a hierarchy of importance and power. From an outsider's perspective, a different culture may appear homogenous. The insider, however, will clearly recognize the significant class distinctions in their own group.

Disability

Disability, like all of the issues addresses in this chapter, presents us with difference. When we encounter people who are different from us, we can respond with interest, curiosity, and an eagerness to learn from their other perspective. This generally works well as long as we do not feel threatened by their difference. If it appears that this different sort of person may take control, or confront us with some problematic areas of ourselves, then our feelings are less of curiosity and more of defensiveness. Disability may confront us with our physical limitations, vulnerabilities and mortality. It can exert control over relationships and social interactions. It has enormous power to disturb and disrupt, in the PD group as well as in other areas of life.

Paul is a large man with severe mobility and breathing problems. He moves slowly with the help of a frame and it takes him much longer than the rest of the student group to make the room changes that the college timetable demands. The group have to wait for him regularly and his strained breathing is often noticeable.

a.   How does this new information fit with the image you have so far created? Does it introduce any new emotional reactions?

b.   The group may be impeccably politically correct, but you do not have to be. Beneath the polite surface, whom do you think might be irritated? Who do you imagine taking on a maternal, protective role? In other words, where are the allies and antagonists in your imaginary group?

We are all members of multiple groups simultaneously. Gender, sexuality, class, race, ethnicity, age, ability, all intersect and interact to create a complex position. In reality, it is impossible to separate out these dimensions of our group memberships. Some group memberships confer more advantages than others, so that, for example, Margaret may be disadvantaged because of her age and gender, but advantaged through ethnicity and class.

All of these major themes of gender and sexuality, age, race and ethnicity, social class and disability can be seen metaphorically as fissures or jagged outcrops in the seabed. They lie beneath the surface, sometimes at great depth, playing a powerful role in determining the nature of the sea above. The discussion here touches upon them all lightly, and is in no way a comprehensive exploration.

The purpose is to demonstrate that these issues, which often become the taboo areas in PD group life, are always present and always potent.

Difference and power

They are always present because they represent the divisions and categories that human society constructs in order to survive. There is a limit to our capacity to think and organise and we need to deal with the overwhelming amount of available information by drawing lines and dividing it up into groups. We divide the world into us and them, and then subdivide the divisions into manageable parcels. Belonging to a group brings identity and some security, both of which are prerequisites for human survival. The groups that this chapter has been looking at are the fundamental categories into which humans have organised themselves.

Divisions are not only necessary for organising the overwhelming amount of data but are crucial in the battle for limited resources. The group that can control the land or the water has not only the means to survive but can dictate terms to those who do not. In any discussion of division and difference, it is important to recognise the integral factor of power. Difference is not benign or neutral. It is there for a reason and that reason says something about power. Class, race, gender—all the categories of this chapter, demarcate the advantaged from the disadvantaged, the powerful from the less powerful. Oppression, coercion, silencing, and marginalizing are the overt tools for maintaining the hierarchy. The most effective tool, however, is the belief that none of this is taking place, and that things are in their rightful order. Here we come back to the ways in which we are structured by the society we grow into. By the time we have the capacity to question the universe we inhabit, this process has already taken place and is part of us. The challenge then, is to become aware of the internalised framework.

The members of the PD group may all as individuals lead ethical, socially responsible lives, and do their utmost to treat their fellow humans with respect and fairness. Nevertheless there will always be areas of themselves that they cannot see, which will harbour the patternings of their culture and society. A genuine recognition of this represents an important achievement in the process of personal development. No therapist wants to see her or himself as an intrinsic part of an unjust system, but there is always a gap between who we would like to be and who we are in the world

It is much easier to recognise these structures of power from the position of the disadvantaged group. Those who are marginalized lead the struggle to gain recognition and justice. The changing views of women in this society have been generated by women themselves, the increasing recognition of disability has been brought about by the disabled, and so forth. It is much easier to feel the weight of oppression of any sort than to recognise oneself in the role of oppressor.

Group members can be sharply aware of the prejudice that is directed towards them. Some times their own experience of discrimination enables them to be highly sensitive to situations where others are being similarly treated, and to challenge this behaviour. This is not always the case, however. Neither is it inevitable that being victimised gives any insight into one's own prejudices and discriminatory behaviour.

Each of the following sentences refers to a perceived attitude or prejudice that is expressed in the group. They have been gathered together from a number of group sessions, not from one particular group meeting. The task is to reflect upon the unseen. Take each member in turn and note what it is that they see in other members. Do you think that there is some prejudice that they have not seen in themselves?

Jan confronts Margaret about her attitude to Vinnie, which she sees as homophobic.

Gloria gets angry with Irma, and the conflict culminates in Gloria saying that Irma is a racist.

Vinnie thinks Gloria is judgmental about his sexuality, and Gloria tells him that homosexuality is a sin.

Joanne doesn't like the way that Vinnie talks to Sheena. She thinks he belittles her contributions.

Irma says that Paul is always trying to get David on his side.

Jan says she finds Margaret's upper class accent very irritating.

Sheena says that Jan seems to find a lot of things about Margaret irritating.

Paul says that Joanne hasn't got a sense of humour.

Margaret and Vinnie agree that David is very insightful.

Joanne says that she experiences Paul as sexist.

Paul says he is being scapegoated as the only heterosexual man in the group

All of this is demanding and challenging work. Often a PD group decides, either explicitly or covertly, that this is part of the sea where the currents are too dangerous and difficult, and rows off in a different direction. It may go in search of a safe harbour where there is shelter from the stormy waters of discrimination, prejudice, oppression, and injustice. This is an understandable response. There seems no resolution to the sort of conflicts that this chapter has been acknowledging. All of them can confront us with a great sense of hopelessness and impotence.

CHAPTER NINE

Ways of understanding

One of the ways in which we try to deal with the sense of hopelessness is to understand more about what is happening. This chapter looks at some of the concepts that have been developed to increase our intellectual grasp of the underlying divisions and conflicts that all societies share.

The scapegoat

Whenever the PD group is struggling with the powerful themes of conflict and division, the word "scapegoat" is likely to be heard above the rough seas. It is the one "group concept" that everyone has heard of, and maybe as a result, is frequently misapplied.

The original "scapegoat" of the Old Testament was sent into the wilderness, carrying the sins of the community. The goat took with it the bad parts of the group, leaving only the good in a rejuvenated, cleansed society. This worked well until just by virtue of living, things got messy again, and another goat was needed to get rid of the rubbish. There was also a good goat, whose fate was to be sacrificed to the Lord. The devil had one goat, God had the other, and in this way good and bad were split apart and dealt with. The polarisation of good and bad is a powerful and continuous dynamic in society, and thus also in the PD group.

The "good goat" is less evident in PD groups, but the belief that underpins the scapegoat story is always present. This is the primitive conviction that it is possible to get rid of unwanted parts, of the self and of the group, by finding or attributing them in a group member who can then be expelled. Within our society, for example, asylum seekers have been held responsible for high levels of crime and unemployment, and the popular solution is expulsion. If all the asylum seekers were to be expelled, then of course the problems of crime and employment are not resolved in any permanent way. Sooner or later, another group will be accused of causing these difficulties, and there will be cries for their expulsion too.

One goat is sent into the wilderness, followed by a brief period of relief and then another goat emerges. The process repeats and repeats. Within a PD group, for example, a member may be accused of defensiveness, lack of engagement, rigidity, and a refusal or inability to reflect upon themselves. When all challenges fail, the solution is for them to leave the group. The focus will then turn to another member who appears to behave in a similar way, and this will be repeated until there are either no members left in the group, or the group as a whole can work on the issues of defensiveness, etc. Only when the group members can begin to acknowledge that they all contribute to the problems in question will the cycle be broken.

So if the word "scapegoat" appears within the group, one question to be looked at concerns the nature of the challenge or accusation and its distribution around the group circle. Is one member being accused of some group crime and all other members are innocent? This is the process of splitting, whereby we disown aspects of ourselves and attribute them to another. Perhaps an example from the group we have been looking at will help to make this clear.

Joanne: (Angrily) Well I've tried and tried with you Paul, but I can never get close to you. I would really like to get to know you but it feels as if you are behind a glass wall. I can see you but can't touch.

Paul: (Angrily) Just because I won't say the things you want me to say, you get mad. There are private bits of my life and that's that. You're just nosey; you are always pecking and prying away at people to tell you all the juicy bits. That's your problem.

How do the group react to this emotionally charged conflict? If the group respond by unanimously supporting either member, a closer investigation is called for. The group could have stopped rowing and started to play "Pass the Parcel". The parcel containing "difficulties with intimacy" can be sent around the group to sit on Paul's lap and he ends up with everybody's parcels piled high upon his chair. Or the parcels containing "invasiveness and control" can flow around the group, ending up on Joanne's chair. Diagrammatically it would look as if all the flow in the group was directed to one particular member.

This dynamic occurs often, especially in the early stages of the PD group, and is part of the normal working of the group. As members learn to reclaim their own parcels and work on them, it occurs less and lasts fleetingly. In itself it does not define scapegoating

Scapegoating has a particular emotional character. The passion and intensity of feeling is an important element in identifying when "pass the parcel" moves into scapegoating. All of the group members appear to be caught up in a powerful wave of shared emotion focused upon one member. It can feel like a pack pursuing its prey, with everyone swept up into the drama, including at times the facilitator. This intense, primitive feeling, which leaves no space for self-reflection, marks out the phenomena of scapegoating from other types of group behaviour.

The facilitator should hopefully be one of the first people in the group to be able to escape the emotional pull and begin to think, helping the group to reclaim its balance.

Sometimes it is a group member who can resist the magnetic force and begin to reflect upon her or his own experience. Then the group can begin to move. When members are pulling on their own oars, there is rarely the passion and never the unanimity that scapegoating produces.

Usually when group members complain that they are being scapegoated, they see themselves as innocent in the same way that the goat is in the original story. Here the animal is chosen at random and is in no way complicit. It just happens to be a goat. So when Paul complains that he has been made the scapegoat, he says that bad feelings have been projected onto him for no reason other than that he just happens to be a heterosexual male.

This is one of the most challenging scenarios in PD group life. Is the scapegoat an innocent victim, or are they in any way complicit in the dynamic? Paul can be seen as a defended and emotionally self-contained individual who needs to open up in the group. He can also be seen as a representative of the male stereotype in which emotional self-disclosure is not the characteristic style of relating. The conflict between Joanne and Paul is the conflict between men and women that has been going on for all time—the emotionally demanding and expressive female and the closed, rational male. All the frustrations of centuries may lie behind what is taking place in the here and now of the group.

Is Paul using the scapegoat argument to deny any problems with his own behaviour? Given that he has chosen to be on a counselling or psychotherapy course, is his defensiveness provocative? Or are the group denying the underlying importance of gender division and conflict?

But of course that is not all. There is another crucial difference so far overlooked, and that is disability. Paul sits in the group not only as the advantaged white heterosexual male, but also as the disabled person. Expelling the less able from the group has a very long history in society also. Somewhere in the complexities of the group conflict there will be underlying attitudes to disability to catch sight of and acknowledge.

Some of the most difficult group situations arise when someone is "innocent" in being cast in a cultural scapegoat role, through skin colour or disability, for example, but also "complicit" in that there is some unconscious invitation to play out this victim/persecutor pattern. Group members who perceive themselves to be badly treated in life, and who have experienced groups as places where they are attacked and rejected, may in largely unconscious ways provoke the group to conform to their blueprint. With enough pressure the group will probably play its allotted part, and it can be extremely difficult to unlock this victim/persecutor/rescuer pattern. Any challenge becomes construed as persecution, and all communication becomes cast into an inflexible mould shaped by early experience. So that— "I'm being made the scapegoat in this group" means—"Once again I am the victim and you are the persecutor".

A better understanding the phenomena of scapegoating enables group members to question their own emotions and behaviour. It is a word that describes a particular moment in group behaviour that is often is misused. Even when is it accurately applied, it only describes rather than explains. There are always further questions to be asked about the powerful communication of emotion and sensation within the group.

Pass the parcels

Scapegoating belongs to a family of concepts drawn from psycho-dynamic theory that attempt to chart and explain the ways in which feelings seem to travel from one person to another. They are largely the product of work in individual therapies and do not always have great explanatory power in a group setting. One of the major limitations is that they start with the separate individual and then puzzle over the complexities of how these individuals communicate. Starting with the group rather than the individual leads into an appreciation of the shared communicative space that we all inhabit. This forms part of the discussion in the first chapter. From this perspective, it is no surprise that emotions do not sit tidily upon their own chair in the group.

However, the complexity of group processes mean that we can usefully think about what is happening in both ways. On the one hand, we inhabit a shared pool of emotion, and on the other we are quite capable of sending each other parcels above the water line. "Pass the parcel" featured in the above account of scapegoating and has in many ways infiltrated itself into vignettes through out the book. At its simplest, it describes the process whereby we attribute to emotions or attitudes to another person that are, once unwrapped, identifiable as part of ourselves. We attribute them to others because we are uncomfortable with them and it troubles us to think of them as aspects of ourselves.

Pat had hoped to get to the library in the break between classes, but somehow Lesley had organised her into a meeting with Judy and Ian to discuss the assignment. When she got to the room, Lesley was already talking to Ian in a very animated way about Judy.

"She is just impossible to organise. Whenever I suggest a meeting she always has a reason why she can't come. She's just a control freak, that's what I think. It always has to be on her terms!"

Parcels are not necessarily full of negatives. Some people are full of admiration for another and fail to appreciate their own strengths. Hero or heroine worship is an example of "pass-the-parcel" where the other is perceived in unrealistic terms, and the self is denigrated by comparison. Accepting strengths can be as problematic as accepting weaknesses and offers another example where some unwrapping would be productive.

There is a further development in the story when the recipient believes that the parcel truly belongs to them. If Judy, in the example above, came to believe that she was indeed a control freak, then she has unwrapped Lesley's parcel and accepted it as her own. However, it is wise to be suspicious of any account that attributes the entire contents of the parcel to one person. Parcels are usually carefully if unconsciously targeted. We send them to particular people because we recognise something of their suitability to hold our parcel. Unwrapping will usually reveal that both sender and recipient are implicated in the contents, whatever that may be.

Transference

Transference is a particular sort of parcel. Here we are not just sending an emotion or attitude, but a whole configuration. Instead of perceiving the other as having some characteristic that we wish to disown, we see them as if they are familiar people from our own history. Again, there have been many examples in the book where this has taken place without being named as "transference". The problem with the word, as with "scapegoat", is that it is too easy to assume that having given it a name we have found the explanation and need think no further.

Transference describes the way in which we construct a distorted picture without our conscious awareness. We create a whole person out of fragments of information and perception and then proceed to relate to the image that we have constructed. It is an inevitable outcome of our mental process that continuously predicts behaviour and outcomes from a small number of cues. The label "transference" is reserved for the field of psychotherapy and counselling but the process is universal and exists in all relationships.

Being recognised and loved for "who we are" rather than the other's construction of us is again another universal desire, which is articulated in the world of therapy as "relating at meaningful depth". The aim is to get beyond our continuous constructions of the other to meet in Martin Buber's terms as "I" and "Thou". This struggle is at the centre of any well functioning PD group, which will be engaged in trying to identify and transform the multilayered transferences that are alive in the room.

In a one-to-one counselling or psychotherapy relationship, the idea is that the therapist is as aware as possible of their own transferences and can free the relational space to concentrate upon those of the client. But as these are unconscious processes, even the most self aware therapist will at times be caught in the tangle of misperceptions. Supervision then provides the vital third perspective to help disentangle therapist and client.

There is far greater scope for getting tied in knots in the group situation where the relationships are multiplied exponentially. But at the same time, many different perspectives can exist in the group, all providing alternative and challenging perceptions. Group members can play a similar role for each other as the supervisor does for the individual therapist.

Heather had come to the point of making sure she never sat next to Lee in the group. Earlier in the group he had challenged her about her relationship with another group member, Elaine. He found it irritating, he had said, that she always let Elaine do the talking. Why wouldn't she deal with him directly? She had said something about being a shy person and he had laughed at her, telling her that was such a pathetic excuse. She had felt the anger and sense of injustice well up inside of her and was determined not to let him see how upset she was.

The more she watched him operate on the course and in the group, the more convinced she became that he was rigid and insensitive, perhaps even cruel.

If this became a conversation in the group rather than in Heather's mind, it would become possible to compare her perceptions with those of other group members. She might discover that Patrick thought of Lee as a very sensitive and caring person; that Shabbir was also frustrated by the way she hid behind Elaine; that Emma thought Lee hid his real feelings beneath an act of being indifferent; that Helen had thought Heather's comment about being shy was a way of brushing off Lee's attempt to engage with her and that he had been hurt; and so forth.

If all this did not shake Heather's conviction that her perceptions were correct then she has to answer the next obvious question. "Who" is this insensitive rigid and cruel person that she perceives Lee to be? In the eyes of the group, Lee does not fit this part, so who is he being mistaken for?

It is important to remember that transferences are brought to life in particular contexts. It is quite possible that Heather and Lee could have met in other circumstances and had a different relationship. The context of the PD group brings to life certain unconscious or partly conscious patterns depending on the unique characteristics of the particular group. There will be other significant ingredients present in the group that will enable this particular parcel to be made up. Other members will have contributed all sorts of bits of wrapping paper and pieces of string that will not necessarily be obvious at the outset. Even if it never becomes clear, transferences in the group are not simply dyadic processes. They are "part and parcel" of the group.

Mirroring

Another idea used to understand these interpersonal processes is that of "mirroring". This is a concept that has been taken up by some group theorists because it incorporates the network of relationships rather than necessarily focusing on a dyad.

Just as we need some form of reflection to see our physical selves and to build an internal image of how we look, we need reflections to develop the sense of our inner selves. The group is seen as a "hall of mirrors" within which members both act as mirrors for each other and can catch sight of themselves and others from multiple perspectives.

Sara finds Rosie difficult in the group, particularly when Rosie is talking in her "counsellor voice" as Sara calls it. It is all too sickly, she thinks. There are no hard edges to Rosie—everything is gentle and considerate and nice. At some stage she feeds this back carefully to Rosie, who looks flushed but listens attentively, head on one side. Rosie acknowledges that perhaps she finds it difficult to be confrontational but then thinks everyone should treat people considerately and respectfully.

Sara nods in agreement and shuts up. Krista then points out how Sara has just "rolled over". Where is the fight in Sara? Krista thinks it's hard to find anything sharp in Sara too. In fact, she wonders if thy both compete for the empathy prize in the group. Both Sara and Rosie deny this emphatically.

Rosie holds up a mirror that can enable Sara to see her own difficulties with softness and hardness, and vice versa. Krista's mirror can enable them to look at the issue of competitiveness, probably because it is an important aspect of Krista that is becoming visible also. One particular aspect can be seen and then worked upon using one mirror, whilst other parts of the self are made visible in other mirrors. Each member can reflect back a variety of images and can catch sight of the multiple dimensions of their own "self".

In this way it is a concept that helps to move away from a unitary version of the self. Each group member is a complex inter-relationship of selves that engage in the process of relating with other member's multiple selves. This is not a version of multiple personality disorder, but rather a view of the person as made up of a number of related aspects. Probably the most familiar example of this would be the distinction that is often drawn between the adult and the child self. Most people can recognise that although adults, they can behave at times as a child, and the phrase "the inner child" is widely used. Within the PD group it will be possible to catch sight of a number of these "inner children" at some point in the journey.

The internal group

The child/adult distinction usually breaks down when it fails to capture the more subtle variations in mood and behaviour. At this point it becomes valuable to introduce more characters—parent is the obvious one, but there are many others. An inner ballerina, judge, car mechanic, fluffy toy, grumpy old man, wicked witch, celebrity, earth mother—a wonderfully overflowing cast of imaginative characters that each person carries around with them.

This is the inner group, with quiet and noisy characters, some hiding in the corners, some trying to control and others keeping a low profile. Somewhat like a PD group, you might think.

Getting to know your own internal group is another valuable route to self-understanding. It also provides a way of under-standing the interactions in the PD group that does not rely upon the "pass-the-parcel" type analogy. Your internal "bossy sister" may develop a conversation with someone else's "poor me" sitting across the circle. Another group member's "fairy godmother" might spring to the rescue of "poor me", and then later reveal their own "Cinderella".

Construct your own list of internal characters. Imagine you are asked to make a film to demonstrate the various aspects of your personality, and draw up a cast list.

There will be some obvious characters, who perhaps take leading roles, and some with smaller parts. Or perhaps the quiet, behind-the-scenes characters are in fact more powerful that at first they might appear. As in any good film, expect there to be a range of characters and moods with both darkness and light.

As the work of the PD group gets under way, it becomes more possible to observe these interactions as well as act them out. Personal development encourages the growth of an aspect of the self that is able to stand apart and look at what is happening—not to other people but to oneself. This is an important internal character that becomes able to see the bigger picture whilst the others are engrossed in their own scripts. Through this character, the other parts can be held in relation to each other and better integrated.

One of the tasks will be to encourage the various internal group members to communicate with each other. Everyone needs their voice to be heard in the internal group as much as the external group. Certain characters will need to be restrained in order to hear the others. The children need their views listened to without necessarily having control. They need to be contained and kept safe whilst the adults take important decisions. All this is the work of the internal facilitator, that aspect of the self that can stand apart and appreciate the larger perspective. Both the internal and the external groups need facilitating effectively.

This parallel between a member's internal group and the working of the PD group leads into another important way of understanding. Systemic thinking underlines the parallel processes and inter-relationships of internal and external, individual and group, group and context, context and society.

Systemic thinking

Throughout the book there have been examples of the connections between what is happening in the individual group member, what is happening in the group as a whole, and what is going on in the course and the wider system of the institution.

To think systemically is to reflect upon the ways in which these concentric or overlapping networks might interact and mirror each other. The PD group can be thought of as a system that operates with certain spoken and unspoken rules and that has characteristic patterns of behaviour. An individual is another system, with spoken and unspoken rules and characteristic patterns of behaviour. A family is a system, and so too is a college, or a course within a college. All of these systems exist in relationship to each other, with a continuous and usually unseen flow of information passing from one system to another.

This information flow lies behind the concept of "parallel process". This is perhaps one of the more familiar examples of systemic thinking that is used within counselling and psychotherapy supervision. In a supervision session, certain patterns are experienced and identified that can be directly linked to ones that are operating in the counselling room. These patterns in turn can be seen in the clients' life and network of relationships and are also operating within the system that is the client's internal world—the intrapsychic system.

Here is another example set in the context of counselling training where there are at least five systems operating simultaneously.

Julian was a first year student who was aware of a nagging voice in his head that seemed to criticise whatever he did. His internal group was dominated by this one character who would not let the others take up any space.

His PD group seemed taken over by a sub group of three older students who always had a lot to say about the poor quality of the teaching facilities.

The staff team did not often meet as a whole group because they could not manage the conflict between two outspoken members.

The departmental head was a forbidding figure with an authoritarian style. Departmental meetings were used to pass on his latest instructions rather than as a forum for discussion.

The college principal had adopted a successful "divide and rule" strategy that prevented any group uniting against him.

In all probability Julian is completely unaware that in joining the course he has become part of a context in which the "group" is disabled at all levels. Throughout most of this hierarchical structure, there is an absence of shared consensual decision making. Most voices are silenced whilst one or two hold the power. Julian may only be able to see the smaller picture but he will experience the impact of this overall systemic pattern.

In this situation the PD group has an uphill struggle, trying to work against the grain of the institution to create a space in which all voices can be heard and valued. It helps to appreciate that they are battling, not just with the inherent challenges of group life, but also with a pervasive institutional force. The dominant system can to some extent be resisted once it is identified as a major factor in the life of the PD group. Some counselling and psychotherapy courses are themselves small pockets of resistance within their institutional system that keep alive a different set of ideals and values.

If the PD group can become a place in which all the voices can be heard then students can develop a corresponding ability to listen to all their own internal voices. Just as the members in the PD group can learn to communicate with each other, so to can the internal voices. It is a task of integration in which various aspects are distinct but in communication with each other. Parts are neither separated nor rigidly locked together, but linked in a loose and flexible configuration. All of the voices have a valuable role to play and the opportunity to contribute to the whole. The person who speaks with only one voice usually does so because some internal character has grabbed the megaphone, not because they have achieved a healthy internal balance.

Having identified the characters in your internal group, imagine them sitting in a circle with the task of communicating with each other. Who will speak the most and who will try to hide? How might it feel to be in this group? What might help this group to communicate better with each other? Give yourself the voice of facilitator and imagine what you might say.

Can you find any parallels between your own internal group and the PD group?

Further ideas

These ways of understanding what is happening in the group are a useful beginning and will give most students enough to make better use of their PD group experience. For those who find themselves increasingly interested in groupwork, there is a wealth of material from different approaches. A good place to start might be with these four helpful texts.

Barnes, W.R., Ernst, S. and Hyde, K. (1999). *An Introduction to Groupwork: A group-Analytic Perspective*. London: Macmillan.
Lago, C. and MacMillan, M. (1999). *Experiences in relatedness: Groupwork and the "Person-centred approach"*. Ross-on-Wye: PCCS Books.
Yalom, I. (1995). *The Theory and Practice of Group Psychotherapy*. New York: Basic Books.
Whitaker, D.S. (1989). *Using Groups to Help People*. London: Routledge.

CHAPTER TEN

Authority

The issue of authority is such a significant part of the PD group, both in content and process, because it is such an important concern in life. Who are the people who can tell us what to do, and how do they have this power? Is authority always abusive? Can we get rid of authority? Can we evade or subvert authority? How do we develop our own sense of authority? What sort of authority might we become?

Authority is power, and those issues that were discussed earlier in the book concerning power in society cannot be laid aside, but need to underpin our understanding. Here we are looking at it from a different angle, coming up from the depths to examine the more clearly visible gulf stream of authority that the group boat must navigate.

At this point in the journey, it usually becomes apparent that the boat is carrying a great deal of luggage. The cumulative past experiences of authority pile up in the hold, and need attention. Too much luggage can weigh the boat down in the water and impede its progress.

Parents and authority

The PD group begins with the idea of adult members. All of the group have made adult choices to be there, and accept that they have responsibility for their own growth and development. Most students, however, can recognise within themselves a richer and more complex range of internal voices, characters, and configurations. The adult is not the only person sitting in the group circle.

In every group journey, there are recurrent patterns of turbulence that swirl around the sea of parenting. The foundational experiences of being a child in the family shape every PD group member, however much they feel they have developed an independent adult self. Children have very varied experiences of authority, which change through generations and patterns of child rearing. They inhabit a world of parents, carers, and teachers, who generally have or try to have some control over their behaviour. Reactions and attitudes to these authority figures become internalised into patterns that can play themselves out again and again in adult situations, with managers, tutors, bosses, police, local officials and so on.

Imagine that inside every "mature adult" there is rebellious adolescent and a vulnerable child. They have different needs that they seek to meet in relationship to parent and authority characters. Put most "mature adults" into a group and very quickly the other characters, the adolescents and the children, will make their presence felt. The adolescents do not want to be told what to do or controlled, but at the same time they want security and need some boundaries. The children want parents who love them and take care of them.

Sometimes the parent figure is perceived to be the group as a whole, sometimes it is a powerful group member, and often it is the facilitator. Whoever has been given the role of parent has the impossible task of meeting all these differing needs and is inevitably going to fail at some point. The result is anger and/or distress.

"Why haven't you looked after me? Why have you let me down? Why don't you tell us what to do? Why do you try to tell us what to do? Why should I follow your rules?"

Much of this goes on beneath the surface, an underlying current not articulated clearly but shaping the group conversation.

Keri was seething, filled with a sense of great injustice. Next week, she told herself, I am going to say something. It's just not good enough and I'm not going to accept it! By the time the next PD group arrived, she had worked herself into an even greater sense of outrage

The group had only been going for a few minutes when she burst out

"I am feeling so angry about last week, and so upset for you, Martin. I feel we really let you down."

Martin looked surprised.

"What do you mean?" asked Deb.

"Martin was trying to tell us something very important and none of us listened properly—and then you (looking at Jim, the facilitator) just changed the subject completely. So Martin's issues were completely ignored and we all talked about what you wanted, not about what was happening in the group. I didn't think that was what facilitators were supposed to do, hijack the group!"

Silence

"I can't quite remember what happened, I'm sorry", said Helen. "Could you remind me, someone?"

Keri looked thunderous.

"Martin said something about his father being an alcoholic—that's right, isn't it Martin?" asked Deb.

"I thought we did respond but Martin didn't want to say any more," said Graeme.

"But Jim did ask us something about the week before and changed the subject" said Sasha—"I remember now"

"Yes" said Keri, "And Martin was just steamrollered!"

"Well, shouldn't Martin be complaining himself if he was steamrollered, as you say?" said Graeme. "Why are you so angry about it, Keri?"

"I'm angry because it doesn't feel safe here if the facilitator is going to impose his own agenda on the group, and because I think we have let Martin down. Isn't that a good reason to feel angry—or should we all just do whatever Jim says?"

Sasha replied, "I think Keri has a right to feel angry, and I have to admit there have been times in the past—I can't remember the details right now— when I've felt that Jim has taken over and redirected us."

Keri nodded fiercely.

Here Keri is accusing both the group and the facilitator of not responding appropriately. The group did not look after Martin, and neither did the facilitator, who in addition is accused of imposing his own agenda on the group. It seems that other group members are not angry in the way that Keri is, and do not all share her perception of events. It is pointless to try to answer any question about who is "right" or "wrong" in this circumstance, but it can be illuminating to think about what factors might be involved.

The criticism seems to be that some responsible body—group or facilitator—has failed to meet the needs of a vulnerable group member. This has generated a highly charged angry response, not from the vulnerable member in question, but from another student in the group. For many people, fighting for the perceived rights of other people has a legitimacy that fighting for oneself does not. The problem here is that if it is not possible to fight for oneself, then other people have to be recruited as worthy causes to do battle for. It looks as if Martin has been enlisted in a fight that has taken him by surprise. It is led by Keri with Sasha in support, whilst Graeme has declined to sign up for it and Martin seems simply bemused.

Something has been triggered in Keri that is obviously powerful, and at this point she is determined to act it out. That is, she perceives the fight to be located in the here and now interaction of the group and is behaving accordingly. There is a neglectful "someone who should be taking better care of Martin", and a "facilitator who is dominating the group, using their power inappropriately and unjustly". And Keri has bravely rolled up her sleeves and challenged them.

The obvious question, voiced in this instance by Graeme, is "where does the passion come from?" Everything that happens in the PD group is there to be used. The task is to explore and understand oneself and others.

In Keri's eyes, the group seems to have undergone a transformation—the picture of a group of adults has become blurred, to be replaced by one in which there are neglected children who need nurture and insensitive bullying parents or authority figures. In old television programmes there was a conventional way of indicating a shift in time, when the picture on the screen began to move in sinuous waves before being replaced by a new scene. There was always a characteristic soundtrack, signalling to the viewer that the story was now moving backwards or forwards in time. Something similar has happened in this group, and the work for both Keri and the rest of the group lies in recognising the transformation from adult to child and adolescent behaviour.

The childlike demand to be cared for and the related protest about lack of nurture is one of the powerful undercurrents that can whip up a storm of anger in the PD group. Being able to sift the past from the present is an enormously demanding task but essential in the course of personal development. It may well be that there is something in the facilitator's behaviour that justifies the challenge and needs to be confronted. It certainly looks as if gender has a significant part to play in the group dynamic. This can only become clear when the present can be released from the stranglehold of past experience. The group needs to work in both dimensions, past and present, to understand what is happening and where the emotion comes from.

A: Think about authority in your own family of origin. Who had power, over what? As a child, whom did you see as the most powerful person?
Looking back, how did you react? For example, were you compliant or rebellious? Were you both of those things in different situations? What made the difference?

B: How did you behave at school? What was your relationship with authority in the school? What was the influence of your peer group? If you were in a peer group, what role did you play for the group? Did that impact upon your relationship with authority?

C: (If you are not a parent, go to the next question.)
As a parent of a young child or children, what sort of authority role did you take up? Was that influenced by your own experiences as a child?
How did you manage your authority with adolescent children? What were/are your strengths and weaknesses?

D: How would you describe your relationship with authority in your employment? Have there been conflicts with managers or supervisors?
Do you have experience of being in authority over others? If so, are you comfortable with this power? Do you find it easy to assert your authority?
What is your style? Do you, for example, insist that people keep to the rules? Do you leave people to find their own ways of working? What feedback do you get/have you had about yourself as an authority figure?

The "mature adult" is a work in progress, rather than a fixed attainable state, and learning about oneself involves identifying and engaging with both childlike and adolescent aspects of the self. There is nothing intrinsically wrong with behaving in childlike ways in the PD group. On the contrary, it is often the route to some significant self-discoveries. The problems only arise when it becomes a characteristic way of behaving that produces no learning, but just repetition.

Approval

To need the approval of others is entirely normal. From birth we are dependent on others and need their attention and care. Unmet needs from infancy and childhood live on in the adult, with results that vary from a desperate search for approval in all relationships, to a resolute self-sufficiency.

In the PD group, one of the tasks is to look again at how approval-seeking and approval-rejecting behaviour shapes our relationships, and to reconsider its role in our adult environment. For many group members, developing a sense of appropriate self worth will mean becoming less dependent on the opinions of others and more confident about their own choices and opinions. For others, it may involve becoming more open to feedback and less self-regarding. These are major tasks in self-development, and the PD group offers a unique environment to explore and adjust the image of self in relation to that held by others.

If the priority in a relationship is to feel approved of then there are whole areas that cannot be explored. No conflict is openly expressed, differences of opinion are suppressed and "being nice" becomes the dominant mode of operation. The "nice" PD group is not likely to be learning much at all.

Some people's approval matters more than others. The opinions of those who we perceive as important, admirable, or influential are more significant than those of people who we perceive to be weak, inadequate, unstable and so on. Those who represent key figures from the past, particularly family members, are likely to have the power to affect us by their approval or disapproval.

That phrase, "to have the power" explains why approval is part of this chapter. In any search for approval, we constrain ourselves in order to please the other. This is a necessary, not pathological, ingredient in relationships. However, if there lacks mutuality—one person needs the approval of someone who does not need his or hers in return, or when the search for approval is the dominating motif in relating, then it does become problematic. Whenever the approval of a particular person or group of people becomes emotionally significant, they become powerful.

Draw a diagram of your PD group as a circle of boxes, using one box to represent each member and the facilitator.

Go round the circle and ask yourself "How important is it that this person likes me?" Rate it on a scale from 1–10, where 10 would mean that it felt very important to be liked by that member, and 1 would indicate that you were indifferent to their attitude towards you.

Now think about those members whose scores are high, asking why their opinion of you is important? Do they, for example, remind you of some significant person in your past?

Does it prevent you from being open about your thoughts and feelings with them?

Imagine yourself as their equal. How would you behave differently?

The authority of the facilitator

The facilitator stands out as one person in the group whose opinion is likely to be of special significance. The role is played out in a multitude of ways depending on the particular person who takes on the part. Although styles and theoretical models vary, there is a universal dynamic whereby each group will at some point attribute authority to the facilitator. This is entirely reasonable, for at one level, the facilitator does both represent and possess authority.

If the facilitator is paid by the institution then however limited other links might be, they can be seen as representatives of the college and/or course. This connection is even stronger if they are a member of the staff team. This is authority by virtue of position, as a teacher may have authority over a pupil. There are multiple attitudes and associations here that can be played out in the PD group.

People also have authority by virtue of their expertise. The facilitator can be viewed as the expert in the group—after all, she or he has been on this journey before in their own training, and must surely be more self aware and have more understanding of the group process. If the facilitator is as clueless as the group members, how can she or he be a useful guide?

In addition, authority is a personal quality. Some people have a certain way of being that leads others to pay attention to what they say and respect their opinions. A strong sense of personal authority is prized in many counselling courses as a positive goal within the training process. Insofar as the facilitator sits in the group as a model of good practice and personal development, then they can be reasonably expected to display this type of authority.

The paradox is that a large part of the work of the PD group centres around the development of authority within the group and its members. The facilitator is continually trying to hand back responsibility to the group for its behaviour, in order that the members can develop their own sense of personal authority. So on the one hand, the facilitator by virtue of expertise and self-awareness is in a position to direct and challenge, and on the other hand they need to sit back and let the group discover things for themselves. This balancing act is one of the key challenges for the facilitator, and as far as the group is concerned he or she will probably never get it right. Like parents, facilitators can never be perfect. Like a parent, the facilitator needs to act authoritatively when there is the risk of destructive and damaging behaviour, but needs to also allow the group to make its own choices and learn from them.

Imagine and describe your ideal PD group facilitator. Make a list of their characteristics.

What is the most important one for you? Why do you think you have chosen this characteristic?

How does the facilitator in you own PD group compare with this imaginary one?

Group members

The facilitator is not the only person in the group who members see as powerful or authoritative. Particular members can seek power, and/or have it given to them, as the PD group travels on its way. As with the facilitator, group members can be accorded authority because of their expertise in a particular area, their connections with other people or institutions that are perceived as powerful, or the sense of personal authority that they convey. These factors justify the claim to authority.

Authority exists in a relationship where there is perceived to be some entitlement to power. The government has the authority to legislate because they have been voted into office. We may be opposed to the way in which they exercise authority but on the whole we accord it some legitimacy. In the PD group, if the facilitator tells the group that there will be a change of venue, then that is likely to be seen as legitimate, and despite grumbles, the group will meet in the new room.

There are different varieties of power, and not all power is authority. For example, group members who consistently mono-polises time and content are powerful but do they have authority?

They may not be seen as having any legitimate entitlement to take up all of the group time, but are nevertheless doing just that. They have seized power, and for some reason the group are not challeng-ing this. Often in these situations PD groups hand responsibility over to facilitators and hope that they will solve the problem. The facilitator may be seen as having legitimate power to challenge the takeover bid, in the way that group members do not.

A lot of PD group time is devoted to power, although it may take some time before it becomes possible to put it into words and discuss it openly. It is a highly charged issue. If it is to be productively explored the group needs to have developed a capacity to navigate turbulent waters. In the meantime, group members compete for time and attention and control of the tiller.

Describing any behaviour in the group as a struggle for power will often be resisted because of the assumption that power is inevitably "bad". It may be hard to accept that everybody tries to assert some level of control over others, but it needs thinking about. Overt bids for total control—"the group will now kneel!"—are not common in PD groups. What is common is a group member dominating the agenda, or blocking the group in its attempt to look at certain issues: Or vying with the facilitator for the most helpful intervention, or forming alliances to press certain attitudes upon the group, or colluding with others who behave in these ways. Every member is implicated in the struggles for determining the agendas and dominant attitudes and assumptions within the group.

Every member arrives in the group with a view of themselves and their relationships that has taken years to perfect. They then proceed to try to enact this in the group setting, which would require all the other members to go along with it. Of course, the beauty of being in a group is that not everyone is prepared to fit in with the other's script, and hence the real possibility for some personal growth. However, few people give up without a fight. The fact that much of this takes place out of awareness does not diminish the tenacity with which all of us hold onto our own beliefs and assumptions and pressure others to conform to our expectations.

The main problem here is not the behaviour itself but denial. If the group members can accept their own desire for power, then the group can work very productively to understand, challenge and modify related behaviour. If there is a dominant attitude that power is a dirty word, and a collusive denial of its operations within the group, the opportunities for growth are stunted.

Draw another circle of boxes to represent your PD group and its members and facilitator. This time rate them according to power. The question is—
"Can I challenge this person?"
1 means "Very easily" and 10 means "Not at all".
When you have completed the exercise compare the results with the earlier exercise about approval.

One of the interesting factors that may come out of this exercise is recognition of the power of vulnerability in a PD group. The member who consistently breaks down in tears whenever anyone challenges him or her may by this behaviour successfully ward off any real engagement with others. The wheelchair user who is fiercely critical of other members may be protected from a counter response because he or she is perceived as more vulnerable than others. In a similar way, group members who are seen as victims of racial discrimination in society can consequently be protected within the group from challenge. A situation can arise where behaviour on the part of certain members is left unchallenged because of fears of increasing the burden of discrimination.

The complexities of power relations in any group are fascinating, and a rich source of learning material if the group can acknowledge their presence and share their fears and desires.

Competition

The PD group has limited resources of time and attention, just like all relationships. If we are to get what we want or need, then we are going to have to find a strategy to deal with this. Competition or co-operation are the obvious solutions.

In the early stages of the PD group there is often an attempt to ward off any threat of competition for resources by creating a structure to share group time equitably. However, competition for time and attention goes on continually in the PD group, above or below the surface. Group members have differing attitudes towards competition and different degrees of skill or comfort as competitors. Some members refuse to compete and take up their familiar position on the edge, whilst other members relish the struggle. Fear of envy can inhibit competition and quench the desire for status. Gender can play a part here too, with competitiveness scoring highly in the stereotypical male's list of positive attributes, and being downplayed in the stereotypical female list.

The compulsive competitor and the stubborn non-competitor both limit their range of interpersonal options. In its balanced form, competition can bring energy and vitality into relationships and into the PD group, and it is more likely to reach this balance if it can be acknowledged in the group and not demonised as destructive behaviour. As the group matures, the fear of competition may become less powerful, and it can become an area to be discussed and learnt from, and even perhaps enjoyed. Out of this can emerge genuine co-operation, rather than a superficial conformity.

How do you react to competition?

1. Your life as a competitor.

On a large sheet of paper draw a line, straight, or curved to represent your life, and divide it into 5-year sections. For each section, answer these questions

Who were my competitors? What was the competition for?

For example, in the 0-5 section, you might think the prize was your mother's attention, and the competitors your father, sibling, and grandmother. In the 15-20 section the competition might be about a leading place in your peer group, with competition from other peers, your best friend, your sister, and so on.

For each answer you have, write it in a balloon and attach it to the relevant section of the lifeline. You can have as many balloons as you can think of for each section.

2. Your style.

What have the experiences above taught you about competition?

How do you respond to it now as an adult?

How does this find its way into your PD group?

The group as a family

The group as a whole comes to be a powerful entity in its own right if the PD group is working well. The PD group becomes a type of family, with some of the universal characteristics of family—lots of ambivalent feelings plus the necessity for commitment and hard work to ensure its optimum functioning. Attachment and dependence are inevitable aspects of important relationships, and can come in negative and positive forms. The relationship with the "group" has all of these elements within it. Members build a relationship with "the group" and nurture and value it, or attack and denigrate it. The feelings, attitudes and behaviours that are triggered in this group relationship open the way to unpacking yet more luggage, which is

...ught into the group from the families of its members. Here again are some valuable possibilities for personal learning.

Families can hold a significant degree of power, and so too can PD groups. One demonstration of its power can be seen in its capacity to make its way into thoughts and emotions of its members well after the actual meeting has finished. It becomes internalised and lives on in the members throughout the week, often with strong emotional resonances.

Another example comes when group members struggle in to college to attend the group on days that otherwise would have been taken as sick leave. They may feel they "ought" to, or that they genuinely want to. A sense of commitment or belonging is a powerful force that can make group attendance a high priority. The member who recognises their own impact upon the group and the responsibility of membership is prepared on occasions to give priority to the needs of the group. In return, the group is prepared at times to put the member's individual needs ahead of those of the group. At its best, it is a reciprocal relationship.

CHAPTER ELEVEN

Putting it into practice

E very PD group will have to travel through some dark and frustrating passages. There will be times when, in the boat metaphor, some members appear to be energetically rowing backwards, with a great deal of splashing but little progress. This chapter looks at some of the most frequently occurring trouble spots, using the ideas that have been discussed throughout the book.

The key is always in the inter-relationship between individual and group. Whenever a group member is splashing water into the boat, the reactions of the other members are an inseparable part of the picture.

In all of these situations, a skilful response by the facilitator may enable the group to proceed. However, the focus here is upon group members and the contributions that they might make towards negotiating these passages. As a consequence, the facilitator has been deliberately sidelined. The groups in these examples cannot afford to sit back and wait for someone else to solve the problem; rather, they all need to pick up their oars and row.

This exercise has a different format. There are a series of vignettes that describe some problematic group situations. Read through them all and then choose at least three situations. Imagine that you are a member of the group in question.

1. How would you feel sitting in the group? What might you say?
2. Imagine reflecting upon the group meeting afterwards. What does your reaction tell you about yourself? Can you make sense of your own response?
3. What might be going on for the group as a whole?
4. What do you imagine is happening for the group member in focus?

The exercise begins with you and your reactions, not with the central character of the vignette. Think about them only when you have explored yourself and the group.

A. *Carol was determined to get as much out of her PD group experience as possible, she told the group. At first it seemed very helpful to have someone in the group with a lot to say. She was lively and amusing, and it was easy to sit back and listen. She was sure that she would make a good counsellor because life had dealt her so many blows and she had survived them all. She dominated each group session and as the weeks wore on, there was an increasing undercurrent of frustration.*

B. *Jane said very little when the group began, and continued in that way. Other group members invited her to join in conversations or asked her opinion, and she would reply with a sentence or two and then fall silent again. Diane complained that Jane was different in the rest of the course and quite capable of joining in if she chose. There was an increasing sense of frustration but Jane made no moves to participate in the group.*

C. *After one challenging group session Maria came back and told the group how upset she had been all week. She announced that she was not prepared to feel so awful and if it ever happened again she had made up her mind to leave the course. She did not wish to discuss the matter any further, she told the group emphatically.*

D. *Richard was the oldest member of the group and had previously been a college lecturer. He was warm and encouraging and skilful at bringing people into the group conversation. He was also very interested in how the group worked and had done a lot of reading. Someone jokingly told him that he should take over from the facilitator.*

E. Tony used the group time to complain about the content of the course, the poor supervision on his placement and the inadequacies and unfairness of the teaching staff. He had become the course representative on the student/staff committee and encouraged other students to voice any complaints or resentments. Whatever the topic of conversation in the group, Tony seemed to find the unfairness and injustice in the situation. He spoke with passion and conviction, and usually the group ended up listening meekly to his point of view.

F. Meera had a lot of problems in her life. The group listened sympathetically and tried to find ways to support Meera. Some of the other group members had problems that were not dissimilar and could offer suggestions based on their own experience. Meera always appeared grateful for the support, but would then go on to explain why any new approach would not work in her particular situation, or that she had tried it already and it had failed. Gradually the other group members realised that whatever their contribution, Meera would always have a reason why it would not be helpful.

G. Hasan was excited about his new placement. His supervisor there, he told the group, was a really good guy and they got on very well. Sometimes they would meet up after work for a coffee to discuss how things were going. Hasan liked his relaxed approach and was full of praise for his supervisor's intuitive skills and supportive attitude. When it came out in the group that they had been discussing clients over coffee, several group members challenged him about the ethics of such behaviour. He was adamant that there was no way anyone could identify the client from the conversation and that there was no problem.

H. Sam was caught up in an ongoing conflict with Georgina. The course had two PD groups, and Georgina was in the "other group" so that it was not possible for them to resolve the conflict within the PD group. Sam's group encouraged her to try again to talk with Georgina, but she did not feel confident enough to tackle Georgina on her own. The group decided that next week, in the PD group time, they would organise a joint meeting of both PD groups to sort out this ongoing conflict.

I. Ruth was very angry. She explained to the group that the tutors had told her that she was not ready to start her placement, but that she had already arranged to see two clients. The counselling agency was run by an ex colleague of hers, Madeline, who knew her well and trusted her. Madeline knew her competence and was happy to let her work with clients, so what was the tutors' problem, she asked?

Once you have thought about these vignettes and done your own work on them, read the following commentaries and compare notes. By now you will hopefully have realised that there are rarely any "right answers", but rather layer upon layer of fascinating possibilities!

A. Carol was determined to get as much out of her PD group experience as possible, she told the group. At first it seemed very helpful to have someone in the group with a lot to say. She was lively and amusing, and it was easy to sit back and listen. She was sure that she would make a good counsellor because life had dealt her so many blows and she had survived them all. She dominated each group session and as the weeks wore on, there was an increasing undercurrent of frustration.

The member who monopolises the group, and the group that allows itself to be monopolised are both partners in a dance. Initially the group makes space for Carol to take the floor, and then feels trapped with the seemingly endless twirls and pirouettes.

Carol presumably is repeating a well-worn pattern of relating, in which the "other" is initially charmed and then irritated. When the "other" finally challenges, Carol will at one level be quite unaware of the hostility she has generated. She may then perceive herself to have been an innocent victim who has been attacked for no reason, so has no motivation to examine her own behaviour. The learning outcome on this path is zero.

The commentary, like the exercise, looks at each of the vignettes from a number of perspectives. The first takes the standpoint of another group member and looks at the possibilities for personal learning that the group situation can produce. The second looks at the situation from a group-as-a whole perspective. Having widened the discussion, the attention only then turns to the group member at the centre of the disturbance.

1. A GROUP MEMBER USES THE SITUATION FOR PERSONAL LEARNING

This was the third group session where Carol had gone on and on about the terrible things her ex partner used to do. Lynne left the group feeling very angry again. Later that evening she thought again about what was happening, not to Carol, but to herself.

"Why am I so angry?" She asked, and "Why don't I say anything?" Gradually she found she had a lot to write in her journal, about her own dominating mother, and about her fears of challenging Carol. Having done some work on her own, she was in a stronger position for the next group meeting, and resolved to do it differently.

Right at the beginning of the group, she spoke about her own experience as a group member over the last few weeks. She was able to explain that what had happened in the group had recreated some of the situations in her childhood with her mother, and in particular had helped her to understand more about her problems in finding a voice. Breaking her own silence was a personal achievement for Lynne, and it also opened the way for other members to share their experiences.

2. THE GROUP ASKS THEMSELVES HOW THEY HAVE CONTRIBUTED TO THE DIFFICULT SITUATION

Another member, Greg, had also felt angry but had done some work on a different aspect—why does the group let this happen? He talked about how it was much more comfortable letting Carol talk and talk, because he could hide away. He wondered if that was what was happening in the group— the group had gone into hiding and set Carol up as the front person. Then it could become her fault that the group was not working properly, and they could all get angry with her instead of taking responsibility for their own lack of contributions.

Greg reflected that Carol had talked a lot about other people's anger towards her. Maybe the group picked up some of this underlying aggression. Maybe the group had found itself becoming the aggressive ex partner? Or perhaps the anger belonged to Carol herself and she could not express it directly?

Greg's contribution opened up another possible direction for the group to travel in, and enabled more members to think aloud about how the group was working.

3. THE GROUP ASKS MORE ABOUT THE MEANING OF THE BEHAVIOUR FOR THE MEMBER IN FOCUS

Another member, Josie, had begun to think more about Carol herself. What was it that drove her to talk so much? Was she anxious—sometimes people talk to cover up their anxiety, and then if nobody else seems to be joining in they feel more anxious and go into overdrive. Was that happening with Carol?

Or did she think that nobody was listening, so she had to repeat everything and really labour each point? Maybe underneath there was a similarity with Lynne—maybe Carol talked so much because she felt that she did not have a voice that was taken seriously?

The combined impact of Lynne, Josie and Greg's contributions could unlock the silent frustration in the group. It is important that it does not become the occasion for a united outburst of resentment directed at Carol, but that members are thoughtful about their own responsibilities for the situation. Meanwhile, if the group can keep Carol in listening rather than speaking mode, she may also be able to reflect upon the situation and make use of some of the ideas and questions that others contribute.

B. *Jane said very little when the group began, and continued in that way. Other group members invited her to join in conversations or asked her opinion, and she would reply with a sentence or two and then fall silent again. Diane complained that Jane was different in the rest of the course and quite capable of joining in if she chose. There was an increasing sense of frustration but Jane made no moves to participate in the group.*

The same approach can be productively applied to this example. Every group member can ask themselves about the impact that the group situation has upon them, as they experience it in the group, and afterwards. Some personal reflecting often brings to the surface links with other people and places, which can shed light upon the present day experience. The silent withholding style is likely to resonate with previous experiences in relationships and generate powerful responses.

Similarly, every group member can ask questions relating to the group processes involved here. In the dance between individual member and group there are always some interesting steps to observe. Are the group being invited into a persecutory role, nagging Jane to speak? Do the angry attacking feelings that are present in the group come from Jane herself? Is she passively angry, pushing the group into expressing this anger?

What about the group's contribution to the situation? Is it convenient to focus all the exasperation about non-participation upon Jane? Who are the other non-participants and what other material is being silenced in the group?

And lastly, there are the questions concerning Jane's own experience. What is going on for her as she sits silently in the group? The question is not "tell us about yourself" in the sense of personal disclosure. Every member needs to disclose personal material at their own pace, when they choose to. The question is "How does it feel to be sitting in the group silently? How does it feel when others share their frustration?" These are legitimate questions, relating to the here and now experience of the group.

When asked in a genuine spirit of enquiry rather than as a thinly disguised wrapper for irritation, these questions can help Jane look at what is happening to her and the group. But, as with the previous example, the group cannot force either Carol or Jane to alter their pattern of relating. That is their own responsibility, which hopefully they will pick up. If not, the group has to continue to work with the impact on each member and the group as a whole. This can be an ongoing and time consuming issue but still offer opportunities for personal learning.

Sometimes it does seem that a particular member is locked rigidly into a pattern of relating that is not open to modification. Communication in the group relies upon a capacity to listen and take in, plus a capacity to speak and put out. This balance between input and output is the communicative basis for healthy relating. Although hopefully the selection procedures in training courses screen out those who cannot either listen or speak, it is not a foolproof process. PD groups sometimes have to struggle with members who are unable to let go of their own perspectives and opinions, even in the face of conflicting evidence, and/or members who refuse to participate in the give and take of group life. This may raise questions about their capacities as counsellors or psychotherapists that again will need to come into the group conversation if it is to be useful material for personal growth. (Chapter 12)

C. *After one challenging group session Maria came back and told the group how upset she had been all week. She announced that she was not prepared to feel so awful and if it ever happened again she had made up her mind to leave the course. She did not wish to discuss the matter any further, she told the group emphatically.*

Here is another example of a group member threatening to stay locked in one place. The group are left with a mysterious black parcel in their midst that they have been instructed not to talk about or pay attention to. The first response is to reflect upon what that feels like in the group. Maria is free to choose her own words, but not those of others.

Lynne says "I feel as if I must have done something terribly wrong last week. And I can't put it right because Maria won't tell me what I've done wrong. This is really uncomfortable for me"

Greg says, "I feel quite differently. I feel angry, as if I've been told to shut up. As if all the group has been told what it can and can't talk about—like Maria is controlling the agenda and if we don't do as she says, she goes."

Josie says, "I wonder how it felt for Maria. I wonder what exactly she means by 'upset'. Maybe it felt like she was falling apart, for example. I've had that sort of feeling and it's awful. I would want to avoid it as well".

Each member has an opportunity to reflect upon his or her particular response. Guilt, anger, empathy—why do any one of these dominate? Maria's participation in the conversation is not necessary for this sort of personal learning to take place. There is no event in the life of the group that cannot be used to discover something about oneself.

D. *Richard was the oldest member of the group and had previously been a college lecturer. He was warm and encouraging and skilful at bringing people into the group conversation. He was also very interested in how the group worked and had done a lot of reading. Someone jokingly told him that he should take over from the facilitator.*

Maria is trying openly to protect herself from engaging at depth in the group. Richard is achieving the same end through a different route. He has become the unofficial deputy facilitator in the group, at times perhaps taking over the facilitator role completely. In taking this course he may reveal sensitive and empathic aspects of himself as well as competitive and controlling elements. What is kept hidden is the vulnerable person who is frightened to engage on equal terms with others in the group.

Lynne was able to use her experience of Richard in the group to explore her feelings about men in control. "I find it hard to challenge you, Richard—you're such a nice guy. But you're becoming like my Dad. I never feel I really know what's going on for you at any personal level because you're so busy being the parent here. You're acting like the facilitator but really you're just like us—and I've been annoyed by it but just going along with it—as if you really were my parent."

Greg said "I think it's a competition between the facilitator and Richard to see who's in control. Some of us want Richard to win, I think, and some of us want order to be restored and the facilitator to assert themselves."

Josie says "Why is it Richard who is playing that part? What's so hard about being one of the group rather than the leader? Is it a male thing? Does it only feel safe if he's in charge—maybe other people have always turned out to be unreliable, so you have to do it yourself always?"

E. Tony used the group time to complain about the content of the course, the poor supervision on his placement and the inadequacies and unfairness of the teaching staff. He had become the course representative on the student/staff committee and encouraged other students to voice any complaints or resentments. Whatever the topic of conversation in the group, Tony seemed to find the unfairness and injustice in the situation. He spoke with passion and conviction, and usually the group ended up listening meekly to his point of view.

Like Richard, Tony has taken up a position that protects him from any personal intimacy in the group, but he has chosen a different role as the group revolutionary. He also dominates the group at times, and some of the discussion on the monopolising member will be relevant here. In addition there is the very interesting question concerning the relationship between the personal and political, which parallels a wider debate within counselling and psychotherapy. Is there a "personal" Tony that can be peeled apart from the "political" Tony? Is the political passion a smokescreen for personal issues or is it inextricably intertwined with who Tony is?

Any member of Tony's group will be confronted with these questions. Issues of power can be problematic and disturbing, and PD groups often try to steer the boat away from these looming rocks. It is more comfortable to work with the myth that the group has no issues of power and control, or that the wider questions of social justice stop at the door of the PD group room.

Lynne becomes aware of her sense of distance from Tony and her desire to depoliticise him. As a self-reflexive woman, Lynne asks herself why she should feel like that? She recognises in herself a strong sense of futility in challenging the way in which the world is organised. She feel small and hopeless in the face of the injustices that she sees in society and wants to move into the more comfortable territory of friends and family and relationships. She can recognize too that her response to both Richard and Tony is very shaped by gender. In her experience, "men and power" come together to form a frustratingly unchallengeable double act. Is the anger she sometimes feels towards Tony some expression of this?

Greg is very thoughtful too about issues of power. Tony himself is preoccupied with power and its misuse, wanting to attack the existing authority structures in the college.

Greg sees both Richard and Tony making a bid to dominate the group in different ways. In a group with more women than men, he too is thinking aloud about gender, and why it seems to be the men who are in this competition for power in the group. How is he himself implicated in this, and how does it connect with the gender of the facilitator?

Josie is working hard to understand what might be going on for Tony. He seems to perceive himself as a victim of oppression who needs to constantly fight back.

She wonders if he has had experiences in his early life where he was the victim of injustice. Is his current passion a way of working with those early experiences?

If Tony can join in the conversation and look at his own behaviour in an undefensive manner, then together the group can reveal a complex web of experiences, attitudes, patterns, and desires that produce great personal learning. Tony may be relieved of the burden of lone political activist in the group by others picking up and owning some of this passion and desire for change. By exploring the roots of his behaviour he may decrease the emotional distance felt in the group without having to moderate the intensity of his political attitudes. The optimum outcome would be a greater sense of integration in the group—a less isolated position for Tony and his political ideas.

F. Meera had a lot of problems in her life. The group listened sympathetically and tried to find ways to support Meera. Some of the other group members had problems that were not dissimilar and could offer suggestions based on their own experience. Meera always appeared grateful for the support, but would then go on to explain why any new approach would not work in her particular situation, or that she had tried it already and it had failed. Gradually the other group members realised that whatever their contribution, Meera would always have a reason why it would not be helpful.

Meera presents a contrasting picture of someone who puts herself into the centre of the group, yet becomes isolated as the group grows increasingly frustrated with her. On the one hand she is open, vulnerable, and prepared to ask for help. On the other, she has a well-honed defence against any possible change. She has the classic "yes but" response that the group members will become familiar with in any future work as therapists. Even if she never manages to grow in the group, her presence brings to the surface some useful material.

Lynne, for example, is helped to get in touch with some difficult areas of her own. Not only does Meera remind her of a previous colleague with whom she had a disastrous relationship, but again challenges her about the ways in which she contains rather than expresses frustration. The most useful insight, however, came when Lynne recognised her own internal "yes but" response. Like Meera, she too was very resistant to make changes, even though she could recognise their potential benefits.

Greg highlighted this for the group as a whole. "All of us have a bit of Meera in us", he said, "that wants something to get better without us having to do anything". He wondered if there was something like that happening in the group itself. Members complained about the pattern that the group seemed to fall into, but did not change anything. There was always someone prepared to go down the well-worn route of offering advice that Meera could then reject.

Josie wondered how aware Meera was of what she was doing. Even though the group was increasingly clear in its feedback, Josie did not think that Meera could take it on board. "There must be lots of advantages to staying in the same place, even though it's really miserable", she pondered aloud in the group.

G. Hasan was excited about his new placement. His supervisor there, he told the group, was a really good guy and they got on very well. Sometimes they would meet up after work for a coffee to discuss how things were going. Hasan liked his relaxed approach and was full of praise for his supervisor's intuitive skills and supportive attitude. When it came out in the group that they had been discussing clients over coffee, several group members challenged him about the ethics of such behaviour. He was adamant that there was no way anyone could identify the client from the conversation and that there was no problem.

Now the group is moving into the complex currents of ethical behaviours and dilemmas. Hasan does not see himself as having any dilemma whereas for other group members, his behaviour and that of his supervisor are highly questionable. There are two unhelpful developments that might take place here. One takes place if the group demonises Hasan and members cannot look thoughtfully at their own behaviour. Who in the group would challenge their own supervisor about ethical behaviour? Who in the group has seen or heard things that they are unhappy about but have chosen to ignore? The other negative outcome occurs if the group colludes with Hasan and decides that there is nothing to worry about.

Ethical dilemmas are a very real part of professional practice and the group is a good opportunity to try out some of the necessary thinking that ethical practice requires. In addition it prompts a valuable revisiting of the ethical codes to which the course and members subscribe. It is an issue that ideally needs to move beyond the confines of the PD group into the wider realm of the course. The group itself may be able to facilitate this move. A positive outcome would be for Hasan, in the course of the group conversation, to appreciate that the situation was more complex than he had at first realised, and decide to talk with his tutor. If Hasan resists this then there are some personal issues that the PD group can usefully explore, but ultimately this could become one of those matters that cannot be contained within the PD group. At this point it is impossible to ignore the role of facilitator who will have a key part to play in any decision about taking information outside of the group. The original contract in respect of confidentiality becomes relevant at this point also.

H. Sam was caught up in an ongoing conflict with Georgina. The course had two PD groups, and Georgina was in the "other group" so that it was not possible for them to resolve the conflict within the PD group. Sam's group encouraged her to try again to talk with Georgina, but she did not feel confident enough to tackle Georgina on her own. The group decided that next week, in the PD group time, they would organise a joint meeting of both PD groups to sort out this ongoing conflict.

This is another situation that needs to be set in the context of the original framework of the group. Has the course structure provided for these eventualities by having a clear format in which inter group conflicts can be discussed? It would seem that in the example above, there is either no clear structure or the group are ignoring it. They appear to have taken a decision as a group that affects the entire course without consultation. Although the facilitator is deliberately given a low profile in these vignettes, in this case she or he has been completely wiped out of the picture.

How does it feel to be a group member in this situation?

Lynne felt confused in the group and agreed to the proposal, carried along by a wave of energy from other more vociferous members. Afterwards she felt quite disturbed and anxious about what had happened, as if she had behaved badly. This led to reflecting upon her experiences at school and her relationship with authority.

Greg had been one of the active members in the group conversation and had some personal work of his own to do afterwards. It had felt exciting and satisfying at the time, taking responsibility and solving a problem. Now he was more thoughtful about the way in which the group had become apparently so determined and unified. There were other solutions to the problem that did not involve over riding the structure of the PD groups, but these were never really considered. There was a strong and contagious desire to break out of what they had called the "straight jacket" of the two-group structure. It was a powerful challenge to the authority of not only the facilitator but the course as a whole.

Josie wondered why Sam needed the support of the entire group. What could be so frightening about Georgina? It reminded her of the gangs of girls at her secondary school who always did everything together. On reflection, it seemed as if the purpose was to win a battle rather than negotiate a compromise or understand a difference. Josie also wondered if Sam had got lost in the group and her situation had been hijacked for some other purpose. Would Sam really feel pleased with the outcome?

I. Ruth was very angry. She explained to the group that the tutors had told her that she was not ready to start her placement, but that she had already arranged to see two clients. The counselling agency was run by an ex colleague of hers, Madeline, who knew her well and trusted her. Madeline knew her competence and was happy to let her work with clients, so what was the tutors' problem, she asked?

Here the group look as if they are being asked to support Ruth in her conflict with the tutors. It is easy to imagine that if Tony were in the group, he would have been delighted to oblige. "Good" (Madeline) is being set against "bad" (course tutors) and the group is invited to align itself on one side or another of the divide. It can hook into a primitive "them and us" response that leaves little room for thinking but leads directly into confrontation.

Lynne, however, is too thoughtful to fall into the trap. She felt very uncomfortable when Ruth was so angry in the group, caught between sympathizing with Ruth and feeling annoyed with her. It reminded her of family rows when she was expected to always take her mother's side. She knew she had found some of Ruth's contributions to both the group and the course insensitive, and to be honest, she agreed with the tutors. It was too difficult to say that in the group.

Greg was quick to point out the split between course and placement that Ruth was experiencing, and the invitation for the group to underline the split. He wondered about the sort of relationship that existed between course and placement before Ruth arrived, and whether Ruth had been a powerful agent in creating a split, or was the current focal point in an ongoing competition. His comments were helpful in alerting the group to the danger of dividing internally into Ruth's supporters or antagonists, rather than working together to dismantle the battle line between the two camps.

Josie had her own experiences of splitting apart the good from the bad and then discovering that it was not so clear-cut. She spoke in the group about her parents' acrimonious divorce, and how she grew up believing that her father was a compulsive liar. Later in life she discovered that it was her mother who had lied to her about a number of key events, and that there had never been any "good" or "bad" person in the story at all. She wondered if this might have any relevance for Ruth?

All three members worked together in the group to break down the categories of good and bad, competent and incompetent that Ruth had presented the group with. Even if Ruth could only pay lip service to this more complex account, the group had done enough work to escape the trap of simply supporting her in her campaign.

All of these commentaries are partial and hopefully any reader will have found far more in each example to ponder. They demonstrate the seemingly endless questioning and unravelling that can be applied to everything that happens in the group. At some point it becomes impossible to hold the complexity, and the most productive course of action is to let go. Personal learning is a creative process. New understandings need time to be absorbed, to soak in and water the soil. Then at a later point, suddenly something makes sense, and a new seed germinates.

This is perhaps one of the most important types of learning that the PD group experience can facilitate. For both the group and its members, there is a time when it is necessary to stop rowing and rest on the oars. First comes the hard work, and then boat needs to drift for a while, carried along by hidden currents. Being able to recognise when to let go is a vital skill in psychotherapy. The group experience demonstrates that nothing really goes away, but returns at different times in different ways. Issues need paying attention to as far as is possible in the moment and then also need to sink out of sight to be processed at an unconscious level. This is as true for the group as for the individual. Something will emerge in its own time, as long as we can listen to the voices within ourselves and within the group.

CHAPTER TWELVE

Coming to the end

E very life is a process of attaching and letting go. Whether it is to people, places, ideas, emotions or activities, the ebb and flow of engaging and detaching characterizes human experience. The ending of the PD group provides an opportunity for every member to recognize and understand more of her or his own process of engagement and detachment.

As the PD group ends, so too may the course. One ending is usually embedded within another, intensifying the emotional impact. This lived experience of ending gives one of the best opportunities to explore the personal meanings of separation and loss.

The end of the group is a sort of death. The members do not die, of course, but the PD group does. It will never exist again in the same way, even if all the members decide to meet regularly. Once it has lost its context, it will become a different group. This aspect of finality is the one which most disturbs, and which has the power to revive memories and emotions of other significant deaths.

It may seem melodramatic to talk of the ending of a PD group in terms of death. In comparison to any significant personal loss, the ending of the group may seem trivial. The point, however, is not comparison but resonance. Every ending may carry the resonance of previous loss. Events in the present can trigger disproportionate responses, overflowing with emotions of the past. This is why endings in individual therapy are treated carefully and thoughtfully, and this is why the ending of the PD group needs a similar sort of consideration.

Every ending is both a conclusion and a microcosm of the group experience. It cannot be detached from the overall process and a group that has worked well will tackle its ending in a very different style from the one that has struggled. Paradoxically, the struggling group may realise in the face of death that life is worth living, however briefly. The limited and decreasing time can draw out important material that the group has been unable to process before. Issues that have sat in the background, half ignored but unresolved, can now find their way into the centre. This can be a very productive time in the group, generating great emotional depth before the final letting go.

On the other hand, a group that has never really managed to get out of the harbour may well be tempted to give up as the ending approaches. Everyone tidies away their oars and sits passively as the

---

This exercise asks you to reflect upon your own experiences of separation and loss. You might want to write in your journal, draw, or just ponder—or choose whatever style you find most helpful when talking with yourself. Use the questions as prompts but allow yourself to range over any related thoughts or feelings that you come across as you do this work.

What experiences of separation and loss do you bring with you into your PD group?

What have been the important endings in your life?

What has your first family taught you about how to respond to loss?

What are/were their customs and practices for example, around the death of a family member?

Is it acceptable to grieve openly, in what way, for how long?

Is the absent person talked about in the family group? Are the memories shared or kept to oneself?

What makes a "good ending" for you, now?

boat bobs up and down, waiting for the point at which they can all disembark. This is a dispiriting experience especially for the minority of group members who want to stay alive right up to the moment of death. The only consolation is that there is no group experience, however frustrating, that cannot be used for personal learning.

Luggage again

Luggage has inevitably featured very strongly in the PD group journey. (Chapter 3) The sort of luggage that we have been talking about is impossible to leave behind until it has been unpacked again and again. All of those suitcases and trunks and backpacks that the group members bring with them add up to a significant weight in the hold. These will shape the boat's journey in so many ways, right up until its last moments.

The group member who falls ill right at the end of the year and misses the last two groups may, for example, be in the grip of more than a physiological virus. It is a considerable challenge to live through the process of ending, rather than fast-forward to the end itself. Previous life experiences may have taught this member that the challenge was unbearable and that the solution was to get out early.

Avoidance can take less overt forms. The member who retreats into non-participation for the final phase chooses a different style, but is also trying to get to the end without doing the work of ending. When this behaviour can be acknowledged and discussed, then there is the opportunity for personal learning.

For some members, the ending presents an opportunity for intimacy that could not be realised earlier on in the group's life. Knowing that the relationship is time limited can offer the necessary security to emerge from behind the brick wall of defences. Again, this pattern can only be understood in the context of life experiences prior to the group—more luggage, in other words.

Because the experiences of attachment, separation and loss are part of everyone's life story, there is no possibility that the group ending can pass by without generating material for personal reflection. Even if a group member feels that the ending has no impact, this in itself opens up the question of attachment.

Attachment

The threads that connect us to other people are literally life giving. If the newborn baby fails to attach to a person or people who attend to its physical and emotional needs, it will not thrive. The baby arrives ready to engage, equipped with instinctive behaviours and responses that promote attachment. The way in which we are connected up into the web of relationships, the sort of threads that link us to others, shape and define who we are.

This is not just a part of the infant experience but continues throughout adult life. The patterns of attachment learnt in infancy and childhood can repeat themselves again and again. Children who experienced unpredictable and intermittent emotional connection can grow into adults who need constant reassurance and find any separation too painful to tolerate. Those who were constantly rejected in their attempts to connect can become adults who guard themselves against emotional attachment to protect themselves from the pain of possible further rejection.

Anyone working in a therapeutic relationship with others, where attachment and separation are always critical issues, needs to understand something of their own pattern. The group experience can be very helpful here, not only as a space in which to reflect upon the issue but as a lived experience of attachment.

Karen. Four more groups before we finish. I woke up this morning feeling really panicky, that it was all going to end. I can't believe how the last two years have flown by.

Julie. They haven't flown by for me. It's been a long slog and I'm looking forward to it all being over, and getting my life back.

Bill. Me too. I've learnt a lot here about myself, but I'm ready to go.

Dawn. I think it's been really interesting too. I won't exactly miss it, but it has taught me a lot.

Julie. I'm not sure I've got anything out of this group really.

Karen. How can you say that, Julie, after all the things you've shared with us? You've changed so much—I can see such a difference in you from the Julie I first met.

Julie. I don't see that. I feel as if I've done a lot of work and not got anything back. I was thinking about it in the week and wishing I'd done some course where they weren't so hung up on personal development.

Gina. You're sounding quite angry, Julie.

Julie. Yes, I feel angry. I feel as if I've been let down and it's all been a disappointment.

Bill. But I agree with Karen—you have changed, Julie. You've done a lot of work here, and personally, I think it's paid off. And you've certainly been very hard on me—which I didn't like at the time but I can see now was really helpful!

Gina. I feel a bit disappointed too. But I know in a way that's my own fault and I have to take responsibility for that. I did just sit back in the group for ages and let you all get on with it. I really regret it now. But you, Julie, you've always pushed yourself and given a lot in this group. I admire you for that—what more could you have done?

Julie. That upsets me, hearing that. Yes, what more could I have done?

Karen (passing her the tissues). I'm quite scared of how I'll be, out there in the world without this as a back up. It worries me that I might lose all the things I think I've gained. Still, I'll make sure I keep in contact with some of you.

Bill. Hannah, you look quite tearful—what's happening?

Hannah. This talk about "what more could I do" has reminded me so much of my mother's death and how I felt. It seemed so unfair that, after all I did for her she died anyway. It still upsets me, and I can remember talking about it here way back in the early days of the group. And it was Julie who really understood how angry and bitter I felt.

The group members here have attached themselves to the group in different ways that reflect the patterns that they bring with them in their luggage.

Julie was the eldest child in a family where there was a high level of conflict between the parents. Her mother was continually threatening to leave, and did so on occasions, leaving and returning unpredictably. Julie worked hard to please and care for her mother in order to prevent these departures. Eventually, when Julie was 13, mother left the home and children for good.

Here the pattern of attachment is unreliable and it leads to a mixture of anger and anxiety, pushing away from and pulling towards intimacy. The echoes of all this are alive in the group, where Julie works really hard and then feels betrayed because once again she feels abandoned as the group ends.

For Karen, there seems a different underlying anxiety. She is facing a potential panic as the connection she has made with the group becomes unplugged, and she is already planning how to minimise the impact by plugging in to relationships with some individual group members. Her anxiety seems to be more about whether or not she can cope without the umbilical cord—will she be able to breathe on her own? This might relate to a childhood experience of anxious mothering. Mothers too have attachment difficulties and the anxiously attached mother can teach her child that separation is a terror to be avoided at all costs.

Dawn brings yet another pattern into the group. Her early experiences taught her that people were profoundly unreliable and that the most secure attachment was to books. As an intelligent child, she was able to make her way through school and university wrapped in a self-protective cocoon of reading, thinking, and academically achieving. For her, the ending will pass by without an emotional ruffle because there has been no meaningful attachment. She has found the course interesting and intellectually stimulating, and can fully understand why she has made no emotional attachment to the group. She has realised that if she is going to pursue a career in counselling or psychotherapy, she will need some long-term work to address this closed of part of herself.

Now it's your turn.

Take a blank sheet of paper and draw a small stick figure in the centre to represent yourself.

Using the whole sheet of paper, draw other figures, or write names, to represent the emotionally significant people in your life.

Now connect yourself to each figure or name with a line, and on each line write how long the relationship has been in your life.

You should end up with a starburst picture of lines radiating out from the centre to each small stick person or name, with the duration of the connection written along the line. Now reflect upon the results.

1. Is the picture dominated by family relationships, or are friends a significant part?
2. Now think yourself back in time 10 years ago. What are the differences between the two pictures? Who has entered and who has departed?
3. Imagine the picture 5 years ago. Again, who has entered and who has departed?
4. If there have been changes, how have you dealt with the losses or separations?
5. Do you find it easy to walk away from relationships? Do you find letting go difficult? Do you usually initiate endings, or find the other person does?

Go back to the original picture and colour code the lines according to the strength of the emotional connection. Choose three coloured pens, one each for—"very close", "close" and "ambivalent" relationships.

Now think about the relationship between length of connection and strength of connection? Are the strongest always the longest? Are there some lengthy but ambivalent links in your picture?

Finally, what does all this have to do with the PD group? Can you see any links between the explorative work you have just done on your own attachment styles and the way in which you have related to the group as a whole and to particular members?

Evaluation

The last exercise began the process of evaluating the experience of the PD group. Evaluation is an intrinsic part of any considered ending. What was it all about? What did it mean for me and for others? Just as when someone dies we talk about their life and review their history, so the closing of the group brings into focus the nature of the whole experience.

Some courses build in a form of evaluation. Students may have to write a personal statement, complete a form, evaluate each other within the group or comply with whatever requirement the course imposes here. Any requirements should be clear, transparent and discussed right at the start of the group process. (Chapter 3) Although there are different points of view about how much contact there should be between course and PD group, there is an inescapable reality that the course is trying to help develop and then assess therapist competence, and that the PD group is part of that process. To deny it any part in the overall evaluation of student progress is a lost opportunity.

However, regardless of the course requirements in respect of evaluation, the group itself can take on this work. Time needs to be set aside for the process, without falling into the seductive pattern of talking right up until the last session as if nothing was going to change.

The obvious question to ask, given this is called a "personal development" group, is "Have I developed?" There is evidence in learning statements, journals, diaries, and any other forms of self-reflection that a student has used in the course of the group process. Alongside this is the invaluable perspective of others. By now, group members will have hopefully come to appreciate that they are mutually responsible for the group, and interdependent upon each other. It is almost impossible to develop on one's own, so the original "I" centred question will implicate "you" and "us". If the group has developed then the members have developed and vice versa. "Has the group developed" is then another key question in the process of evaluation.

The ability to give sensitive but direct feedback is one if the skills that can be learnt in the group. By this stage then it could be possible for students to say openly to each other how they are experienced, with both positive and negatives. For some groups this will by now be a routine part of their interactions, whilst for others it might still feel like dangerous territory.

Completing the course requirements successfully may encourage a student to think of her or himself as a professional and qualified counsellor or therapist. They may feel licensed to engage with others in this particular form of relationship, in voluntary or paid work. Any evaluation has to keep this firmly in mind. Feedback at the level of "you're a nice person" or "I feel fond of you", however valuable, needs to be complemented by some appraisal of competence and capacity to engage as a counsellor with clients. This is often the most difficult area to talk about, and the group may come to an implicit agreement that this critical conversation is not to be risked.

If this is the case, then there may be no alternative but for individual members to reflect upon these questions outside of the group.

Look around the circle of group members, either in real time or in your imagination, and ask yourself "if I needed a counsellor and had to choose someone here, who would it be?"

The next stage is to look at your shortlist and ask why they have been selected. It may be, for example, that you have chosen someone who you think of as a friend and who is not threatening in any way. Or that you have chosen someone that you feel is similar to yourself. So ask what particular qualities have formed the basis of your selection.

Are there some group members that you definitely would not want to be in a counsellor-client relationship with? What is it that makes you so certain?

Now put yourself in focus. What do you think other group members might say about you as counsellor or therapist? What strengths and weaknesses might they point out?

The spiral of development

We grow unevenly and in fits and starts, returning again and again to particular themes and experiences until we can make sense of them, use them, integrate them into other experiences, digest them, metabolise them into nutrient form. Development can rarely be categorised in a linear style, despite checklists and multiple choice questionnaires designed to squeeze it into a measurable shape. This is just as true of the group as it is of every individual member.

The ending of a group often seems uncannily like the beginning. The same themes find their way into the conversation and the same preoccupations dominate the time. The group that began with talk of weak fathers, for example, is likely to find itself once again on the same topic at the end. It would be mistaken to assume from this that the group has got nowhere. On the contrary, it might show how focused a group has been around its central preoccupations and how determined it is to wrestle with them to the last! In hindsight it can appear that the first session of the group laid down the agenda for the whole group experience.

Development here is indicated by the subtle differences in perspectives and understandings, and by the way in which the group conduct the conversation. If they have reached a stage where the conversation can flow evenly, with all members engaged and participating, then it has developed. Looking at changes in the style of communication and levels of participation can give an indication of the growth in the group. At the same time it points to the development within individual members.

An inconclusive conclusion

This might look as if it will be the section in which all the threads are pulled together and some overall wisdom is clearly stated. Hopefully for those who have used the book, there will already be the recognition that this is not how it will all end. There is no tidy summing up to be done. Every vignette and exercise in the book can be done in a different way and reveal different aspects. There are some informed and intelligent analyses and responses to group situations, but there are few clear cut solutions or answers. Every choice generates another set of possibilities and choices, just as it does in life outside of the group.

This can be frustrating and disappointing. Like Julie in the vignette, some members want a clear reward for their efforts and some straightforward answers, even if the questions are staggeringly complex. A good group ending has to recognize both positive and negatives. The insights gained, the relationships created and strengthened, the times of intimacy and connectedness, set alongside the unsatisfactory struggles, the unproductive silences, and the wounds still festering. Some passages and waterways will have been explored and some not. Some temporary conclusions will have been arrived at, only to be revisited and reworked at a later point in the journey. All is in flux and all is incomplete.

This parallels the group process itself. Within the group, ideas are put forward, worked with, left behind, brought back, modified and polished, broken open and reassembled, filed away, and dusted off time and time again. There are periods of gestation and digestion, as well as times of talking. Sometimes the way forward is to let something go, secure in the knowledge that if it is important, it will find its own way back into the centre. Constantly holding it in mind or worrying at it like a terrier can hinder rather than help. The person who tries to hold all the threads together will very quickly feel overwhelmed in a group. Learning when to let go and float, rather than switch off, is another important skill.

Learning does not stop at the last session, either. Any significant relationship or encounter changes us, whether we wish it or not. Members take away with them an internalised version of the group that can sit on their shoulder and talk with them, or suddenly appear at particular moments. The full impact of the experience is never clear by the last session, just as we cannot see the full significance of any relationship until we have some distance from it. All this takes time to emerge.

The ending of the group is an enforced letting go, but the group member who has been able to use it in the ways that this book suggests will find that it does not finish absolutely. The experience can work away in the background, bringing new insights and realisations. In the foreground, it has hopefully may have taught the members some valuable things about themselves and relationships that can be applied both in personal and professional life.

BIBLIOGRAPHY

Barnes, B., Ernst, S., Hyde, K. (1999). *An Introduction to Groupwork: A Group Analytic Perspective*. London: Macmillan Press.

Behr, H. and Hearst, L. (2005). *Group-Analytic Psychotherapy*. London: Whurr.

Bernard, H. and MacKenzie, B. (1994). *Basics of Group Psychotherapy*. New York: Guilford.

Bion, W. (1961). *Experiences in Groups*. London: Tavistock.

Brown, D. and Zinkin, L. (1994). *The Psyche and the Social World*. London: Routledge.

Chazan, R. (2001). *The Group as Therapist*. London: JKP.

Crossley, N. (1996). *Intersubjectivity: The Fabric of Social Becoming*. London: Sage.

Dalal, F. (1998). *Taking the Group Seriously*. London: Jessica Kingsley.

De Chant, B. (1996). *Women and Group Psychotherapy*. New York: Guilford.

Fairclough, N. (1992). *Discourse and Social Change*. Cambridge: Polity Press.

Foulkes, S.H. and Anthony, E.J. (1957). *Group Psychotherapy: The Psychoanalytic Approach*. London: Karnac, 1984 (reprint).

Frith, C. and Wolpert, D. (2003). *The Neuroscience of Social Interaction: Decoding, Influencing and Imitating the Action of Others*. Oxford: Oxford University Press.

Harwood, I. and Pines, M. (eds) (1998). *Self Experiences in Groups*. London: Jessica Kingsley.

Johnson, S. and Meinhof, U. (eds) (1997). *Language and Masculinity*. Oxford: Blackwell.

Kennard, D., Roberts, J., and Winter, D. (1993). *A Workbook of Group Analytic Interventions*. London: Routledge.

Krause, I. (1998). *Therapy Across Culture*. London: Sage.

153

Lago, C. and MacMillan, M. (1999). *Experiences in Relatedness: Groupwork and the Person-Centred Approach*. Ross-on-Wye: PCCS.

Mitchell, S. (1988). *Relational Concepts in Psychoanalysis: An Integration*. Cambridge: Harvard University Press.

Nitsun, M. (1996). *The Anti-Group: Destructive Forces in the Group and their Creative Potential*. London: Routledge.

Nitsun, M. (2006). *The Group as an Object of Desire*. London: Routledge.

Stacey, R. (2003). *Complexity and Group Processes: A Radically Social Understanding of Individuals*. Hove: Routledge.

Stock, W. (1985). *Using Groups to Help People*. London: Routledge.

Thompson, S. (1999). *The Group Context*. London: Jessica Kingsley.

Tudor, K. (1999). *Group Counselling*. London: Sage.

Wilkins, P. (1997). *Personal and Professional Development for Counsellors*. London: Sage.

Winnicott, D.W. (1980). *Playing and Reality*. London: Penguin.

Winnicott, D.W. (1982). *The Maturational Process and the Facilitating Environment*. London: Hogarth Press.

Wodak, R. (1986). *Language Behavior in Therapy Groups*. Berkeley: University of California Press.

Wodak, R. (ed.) (1997). *Gender and Discourse*. London: Sage.

Yalom, I. (1995). *The Theory and Practice of Group Psychotherapy*. New York: Basic Books.

INDEX